Jack C. Richards & Chuck Sandy

Passages
Third Edition

1

Student's Book
with eBook

CAMBRIDGE
UNIVERSITY PRESS

CAMBRIDGE
UNIVERSITY PRESS

University Printing House, Cambridge CB2 8BS, United Kingdom

One Liberty Plaza, 20th Floor, New York, NY 10006, USA

477 Williamstown Road, Port Melbourne, VIC 3207, Australia

314–321, 3rd Floor, Plot 3, Splendor Forum, Jasola District Centre, New Delhi – 110025, India

103 Penang Road, #05-06/07, Visioncrest Commercial, Singapore 238467

Cambridge University Press is part of the University of Cambridge.

It furthers the University's mission by disseminating knowledge in the pursuit of education, learning and research at the highest international levels of excellence.

www.cambridge.org
Information on this title: www.cambridge.org/9781009040617

© Cambridge University Press 2015

This publication is in copyright. Subject to statutory exception and to the provisions of relevant collective licensing agreements, no reproduction of any part may take place without the written permission of Cambridge University Press.

First published 1998
Second edition 2008
Third edition 2015
Update to Third edition published 2021

20 19 18 17 16 15 14 13 12 11 10

Printed in Poland by Opolgraf

A catalog record for this publication is available from the British Library

ISBN 978-1-009-04061-7 Student's Book 1 with eBook
ISBN 978-1-009-04076-1 Student's Book 1A with eBook
ISBN 978-1-009-04082-2 Student's Book 1B with eBook
ISBN 978-1-009-04086-0 Student's Book 1 with Digital Pack
ISBN 978-1-009-04087-7 Student's Book 1A with Digital Pack
ISBN 978-1-009-04088-4 Student's Book 1B with Digital Pack
ISBN 978-1-107-62725-3 Workbook 1
ISBN 978-1-107-62718-5 Workbook 1A
ISBN 978-1-107-62720-8 Workbook 1B
ISBN 978-1-107-62768-0 Teacher's Edition 1 with Assessment Audio
ISBN 978-1-107-62754-3 Class Audio 1
ISBN 978-1-009-04089-1 Full Contact 1 with Digital Pack
ISBN 978-1-009-04090-7 Full Contact 1A with Digital Pack
ISBN 978-1-009-04091-4 Full Contact 1B with Digital Pack
ISBN 978-1-107-62762-8 DVD 1
ISBN 978-1-107-66626-9 Presentation Plus 1

Additional resources for this publication at cambridgeone.org

Cambridge University Press has no responsibility for the persistence or accuracy of URLs for external or third-party internet websites referred to in this publication, and does not guarantee that any content on such websites is, or will remain, accurate or appropriate. Information regarding prices, travel timetables, and other factual information given in this work is correct at the time of first printing but Cambridge University Press does not guarantee the accuracy of such information thereafter.

Art direction, book design, layout services, and photo research: Q2A / Bill Smith
Audio production: John Marshall Media
Video production: Steadman Productions

Authors' Acknowledgments

A great number of people contributed to the development of *Passages Third Edition*. Particular thanks are owed to the following reviewers and institutions, as their insights and suggestions have helped define the content and format of the third edition:

Paulo A. Machado, Rio de Janeiro, Brazil; Simone C. Wanguestel, Niterói, Brazil; Athiná Arcadinos Leite, **ACBEU**, Salvador, Brazil; Lauren Osowski, **Adult Learning Center**, Nashua, NH, USA; Brenda Victoria, **AIF System**, Santiago, Dominican Republic; Alicia Mitchell-Boncquet, **ALPS Language School**, Seattle, WA, USA; Scott C. Welsh, **Arizona State University**, Tempe, AZ, USA; Silvia Corrêa, **Associação Alumni**, São Paulo, Brazil; Henrick Oprea, **Atlantic Idiomas**, Brasília, Brazil; Márcia Lima, **B.A. English School**, Goiânia, Brazil; Carlos Andrés Mejía Gómez, **BNC Centro Colombo Americano Pereira**, Pereira, Colombia; Tanja Jakimoska, **Brava Training**, Rio de Janeiro, Brazil; Paulo Henrique Gomes de Abreu, **Britannia International English**, Rio de Janeiro, Brazil; Gema Kuri Rodríguez, **Business & English**, Puebla, Mexico; Isabela Villas Boas, **Casa Thomas Jefferson**, Brasília, Brazil; Inara Lúcia Castillo Couto, **CEL-LEP**, São Paulo, Brazil; Ana Cristina Hebling Meira, **Centro Cultural Brasil-Estados Unidos**, Campinas, Brazil; Juliana Costa da Silva, **Centro de Cultura Anglo Americana**, Rio de Janeiro, Brazil; Heriberto Díaz Vázquez **Centro de Investigación y Docencia Económicas**, Mexico City, Mexico; D. L. Dorantes-Salas, **Centro de Investigaciones Biológicas del Noroeste**, La Paz, Mexico; Elizabeth Carolina Llatas Castillo, **Centro Peruano Americano El Cultural**, Trujillo-La Libertad, Peru; Márcia M. A. de Brito, **Chance Language Center**, Rio de Janeiro, Brazil; Rosalinda Heredia, **Colegio Motolinia**, San Juan del Río, Mexico; Maria Regina Pereira Filgueiras, **College Language Center**, Londrina, Brazil; Lino Mendoza Rodriguez, **Compummunicate**, Izúcar de Matamoros, Mexico; Maria Lucia Sciamarelli, **Cultura Inglesa**, Campinas, Brazil; Elisabete Thess, **Cultura Inglesa**, Petrópolis, Brazil; Catarina M. B. Pontes Kruppa, **Cultura Inglesa**, São Paulo, Brazil; Sheila Lima, **Curso Oxford**, Rio de Janeiro, Brazil; Elaine Florencio, Beth Vasconcelos, **English House Corporate**, Rio de Janeiro, Brazil; Vasti Rodrigues e Silva, **Fox Idiomas**, Rio de Janeiro, Brazil; Ricardo Ramos Miguel Cézar, Walter Júnior Ribeiro Silva, **Friends Language Center**, Itapaci, Brazil; Márcia Maria Pedrosa Sá Freire de Souza, **IBEU**, Rio de Janeiro, Brazil; Jerusa Rafael, **IBEUV**, Vitória, Brazil; Lilianne de Souza Oliveira, **ICBEU**, Manaus, Brazil; Liviane Santana Paulino de Carvalho, **ICBEU**, São Luís, Brazil; Manuel Marrufo Vásquez, **iempac Instituto de Enseñanza del Idioma Ingles**, Tequila, Mexico; Nora Aquino, **Instituto de Ciencias y Humanidades Tabasco**, Villahermosa, Mexico; Andrea Grimaldo, **Instituto Laurens**, Monterrey, Mexico; Cenk Aykut, Staci Jenkins, Kristen Okada, **Interactive College of Technology**, Chamblee, GA, USA; Imeen Manahan-Vasquez, Zuania Serrano, **Interactive Learning Systems**, Pasadena, TX, USA; Nicholas J. Jackson, **Jackson English School**, Uruapan, Mexico; Marc L. Cummings, **Jefferson Community and Technical College**, Louisville, KY, USA; Solange Nery Veloso, **Nery e Filho Idiomas**, Rio de Janeiro, Brazil; Tomas Sparano Martins, **Phil Young's English School**, Curitiba, Brazil; Paulo Cezar Lira Torres, **PRIME Language Center**, Vitória, Brazil; Angie Vasconcellos, **Robin English School**, Petrópolis, Brazil; Barbara Raifsnider, **San Diego Community College District**, San Diego, CA, USA; James Drury de Matos Fonseca, **SENAC**, Fortaleza, Brazil; Manoel Fialho da Silva Neto, **SENAC**, Recife, Brazil; Marilyn Ponder, **Tecnológico de Monterrey**, Irapuato, Mexico; Linda M. Holden, **The College of Lake County**, Grayslake, IL, USA; Janaína da Silva Cardoso, **UERJ**, Rio de Janeiro, Brazil; Gustavo Reges Ferreira, Sandlei Moraes de Oliveira, **UFES**, Vitória, Brazil; Nancy Alarcón Mendoza, **UNAM, Facultad de Estudios Superiores Zaragoza**, Mexico City, Mexico; Rosa Awilda López Fernández, **UNAPEC**, Santo Domingo, Dominican Republic; Vera Lúcia Ratide, **Unilínguas**, São Leopoldo, Brazil; Elsa Yolanda Cruz Maldonado, **Universidad Autónoma de Chiapas**, Tapachula, Mexico; Deida Perea, **Universidad Autónoma de Ciudad Juárez**, Ciudad Juárez, Mexico; Gabriela Ladrón de Guevara de León, **Universidad Autónoma de la Ciudad de México**, Mexico City, Mexico; Juan Manuel Ardila Prada, **Universidad Autónoma de Occidente**, Cali, Colombia; Lizzete G. Acosta Cruz, **Universidad Autónoma de Zacatecas**, Fresnillo, Mexico; Ary Guel, Fausto Noriega, Areli Martínez Suaste, **Universidad Autónoma de Zacatecas**, Zacatecas, Mexico; Gabriela Cortés Sánchez, **Universidad Autónoma Metropolitana Azcapotzalco**, Mexico City, Mexico; Secundino Isabeles Flores, Guillermo Guadalupe Duran Garcia, Maria Magdalena Cass Zubiria, **Universidad de Colima**, Colima, Mexico; Alejandro Rodríguez Sánchez, **Universidad del Golfo de México Norte**, Orizaba, Mexico; Fabiola Meneses Argüello, **Universidad La Salle Cancún**, Cancún, Mexico; Claudia Isabel Fierro Castillo, **Universidad Politécnica de Chiapas**, Tuxtla Gutierrez, Mexico; Eduardo Aguirre Rodríguez, M.A. Carolina Labastida Villa, **Universidad Politécnica de Quintana Roo**, Cancún, Mexico; Gabriela de Jesús Aubry González, **Universidad TecMilenio Campus Veracruz**, Boca del Rio, Mexico; Frank Ramírez Marín, **Universidad Veracruzana**, Boca del Río, Mexico.

Additional thanks are owed to Alex Tilbury for revising the Self-assessment charts, Paul MacIntyre for revising the Grammar Plus section, and Karen Kawaguchi for writing the Vocabulary Plus section.

Welcome to Passages!

Congratulations! You have learned the basics; now it's time to raise your English to a whole new level.

Your journey through each unit of **Passages Third Edition** will include a range of activities that will **progressively expand your language ability** in a variety of contexts, including formal and informal communication.

Along the way, you will encounter frequent communication reviews and progress checks that will **systematically consolidate your learning**, while **additional grammar and vocabulary practice** is available whenever you need it in the Grammar Plus and Vocabulary Plus sections in the back of this book.

RAISING YOUR ENGLISH TO A WHOLE NEW LEVEL
Unique features to boost your English proficiency!

STARTING POINT presents new grammar in a variety of real-world contexts.

VOCABULARY expands upon prior knowledge and improves vocabulary building skills.
NEW Vocabulary Plus: extra vocabulary practice when you need it!

GRAMMAR is explored in context and builds on previously encountered structures.
Grammar Plus: extra grammar explanations and practice when you need it!

SPEAKING activities spark lively discussions focusing on interesting and relevant situations.

iv

5 LISTENING
Life in Sydney

A Listen to Maria and Ian talk about life in Sydney. Who seems to enjoy living there more?

B Listen again. Which person has these opinions? Choose Maria, Ian, or both.

	Maria	Ian	Both
1. It's easy to get around Sydney.	☐	☐	☐
2. The beaches are great.	☐	☐	☐
3. The rents are expensive.	☐	☐	☐
4. It's a fun place to live.	☐	☐	☐
5. The restaurants are all expensive.	☐	☐	☐
6. Life is better in a smaller town.	☐	☐	☐

LISTENING activities sharpen essential listening comprehension skills.

6 DISCUSSION
Quality of life

A Rate these quality-of-life issues as very important (2), important (1), or not important (0). Can you add one more to the list?

Quality of Life
- ___ affordable housing
- ___ a variety of restaurants
- ___ beautiful parks
- ___ convenient public transportation
- ___ exciting
- ___ first-clas
- ___ historic n
- ___ low crime

B Pair work Which three issues are the most import considering where to live? Explain why.

"I guess affordable housing and exciting nightlife are the m find a place I could afford that was near someplace fun."

"I know what you mean. But for me, I guess low crime rates I want to live somewhere where I feel safe. I don't mind if

C Class activity Share your answers with your clas mentioned most often?

24 UNIT 3 Exploring new cities

7 WRITING
Brainstorming

Brainstorming means making a list of ideas about a topic. Then you can use this list to come up with a topic sentence and ideas to support it.

A Group work Brainstorm as many ideas as you can to add to the dos and don'ts for living on a budget.

Living on a Tight Bu

Do	Don't
• compare prices	• buy the f
• look for sales	• buy bran
• check ads for used items	• use cred

B Group work Brainstorm dos and don'ts for one of
- getting over a bad cold
- staying safe in a bi

C Read this paragraph about living on a tight budget. T sentence and a similar paragraph about your topic u

Living on a tight budget is easy if you follow som shopping. First of all, you should never buy somethi need to check at least a few other stores and go on don't be in a hurry! If you take your time, you might now, ask a salesperson if there's going to be one so secondhand, items. You can check in the newspape for. Finally, you might get a better price at some sto credit card, so be sure to ask about cash discounts.

D Pair work Exchange brainstorming lists and parag Then answer the questions.
1. How many brainstorming ideas did your partner u chose the best ones?
2. Do you have any questions about your partner's p you disagree with?
3. Can you think of a good title for your partner's pa

WRITING tasks build academic writing skills through step-by-step activities.

7 READING
Cyber-begging

A Pair work Imagine that a stranger asked you for money to help pay off a frivolous debt. Would you help? Tell your partner. Then read the article.

Can you spare a dime for my Gucci bills?

There was a time when Karyn Bosnak couldn't pay a $59.00 bill at the grocery store. She was officially broke. She didn't have enough money to get on the subway, but she looked rich. She was a television producer, earned $900 a week, and had a closetful of designer labels like Gucci and Louis Vuitton. But she also had a $20,221.40 credit card bill and an empty bank account. Karyn decided that it was time for a change. She built a website and simply asked people to help her out by sending her a buck or two.

On the site, Karyn honestly explained her situation, Gucci shoes and all. "If 20,000 people gave me just $1, I'd be home free, and I'm sure there are 20,000 people out there who can afford to give me $1." Amazingly, it worked. Her website was visited by more than a million people. Although most donors just gave a few dollars, one generous donor sent $1,000. She was on TV and in newspapers and magazines. She was offered a book deal and a movie contract. And of course, she was able to pay off her credit card debt.

She also sold her designer clothes on eBay. In her closet, where the Gucci purses once sat, Karyn keeps all the letters that people have sent her.

She's received teddy bears, subscriptions to *Vogue*, Dunkin' Donuts coupons, backpacks, jewelry, cat food, and candles.

It's hard to understand why so many people helped a total stranger pay off her huge credit card bill. Why did they do it? Karyn explains, "I was just honest about what happened; I didn't make up some sob story about saving the world." Her donors think it's funny and original, she argues, and view it less as a charity than as an entertainment site.

Imitators have sprung up all over the Internet, some with outrageously selfish requests like a BMW or a house. Actually, Karyn was not the first person to put up a website asking strangers for money. The practice has a name: "cyber-begging." Most sites receive little traffic and even less cash.

Karyn also had thousands of enemies and critics. People sent her hate mail and scolded her on websites. Karyn says she never lets this anger bother her. "They are probably jealous they didn't think of it," she explains.

Source: "Brother, can you spare a dime for my Gucci bills?" by Janelle Brown, Salon.com

B Read the article again and answer the questions. Then compare your answers with a partner.
1. Why was Karyn in financial trouble?
2. What was her main solution to her problem? What else did she do?
3. Why did so many people respond positively to her website?

C Group work Discuss these questions. Then share your answers with the class.
1. Do you think Karyn was unethical, or was she simply clever?
2. What would you have done if you were Karyn?

LESSON B Information overload 61

READING passages drawn from authentic sources promote critical thinking and analysis.

Passages Third Edition is a two-level course that will open the door to communicating with greater fluency and proficiency, with:

- **more sophisticated** real-world grammar and vocabulary,
- **thought-provoking** discussions and academic writing activities,
- **more challenging** listening and reading comprehension topics.

KEEP MOVING UP!
More support is always available – when and where you need it!

The **WORKBOOK** provides extensive practice of grammar and vocabulary as well as additional reading and writing activities.

The **DIGITAL WORKBOOK** – a digital version of the Workbook – enables your teacher to provide instant feedback on your work.

AUDIO AND VIDEO on Cambridge One allows students to review on their own.

cambridgeone.org

v

Plan of BOOK 1

	FUNCTIONS	GRAMMAR	VOCABULARY
UNIT 1 Friends and family pages 2–9			
A What kind of person are you? B Every family is different.	■ Describing personalities ■ Expressing likes and dislikes ■ Describing personal change ■ Stating advantages and disadvantages	■ Verbs followed by gerunds ■ Noun clauses after *be*	■ Personality collocations ■ Compound family terms
UNIT 2 Mistakes and mysteries pages 10–17			
A Life lessons B I can't explain it!	■ Describing rules and obligations in the past ■ Giving advice about the past ■ Speculating about past events ■ Offering explanations about past events	■ Past modals and phrasal modals of obligation ■ Modals with multiple uses	■ Collocations with *problem* ■ Verbs of belief
UNIT 3 Exploring new cities pages 18–25			
A Popular destinations B My kind of town	■ Describing and giving information about places ■ Stating preferences ■ Presenting contrasting information ■ Categorizing and evaluating issues	■ Defining and non-defining relative clauses ■ Order of modifiers ■ Connecting contrasting ideas	■ Features of cities ■ Compound terms for towns
UNITS 1–3 Communication review pages 26–27			
UNIT 4 Early birds and night owls pages 28–35			
A It's about time! B Tossing and turning	■ Describing routines and habits ■ Giving advice ■ Explaining reasons and conditions ■ Giving interpretations of meaning	■ Reduced time clauses ■ Clauses stating reasons and conditions	■ Phrasal verbs related to energy and sleep ■ Expressions related to sleep
UNIT 5 Communication pages 36–43			
A Making conversation B It's personal.	■ Describing types of conversationalists ■ Talking about appropriate behavior ■ Starting a conversation ■ Making small talk ■ Reporting what someone else has said	■ Infinitive and gerund phrases ■ Reported speech	■ Terms to describe behavior ■ Expressions for reported speech
UNIT 6 What's the real story? pages 44–51			
A That's some story! B Storytelling	■ Presenting information in chronological order ■ Narrating news events ■ Organizing and presenting information	■ Present perfect vs. simple past ■ Present perfect vs. present perfect continuous ■ Adverbs with the simple past and past perfect	■ News events ■ Storytelling expressions
UNITS 4–6 Communication review pages 52–53			

SPEAKING	LISTENING	WRITING	READING
- Finding out what personality traits you have in common with your classmates - Comparing personal profiles - Talking about how you have changed or how you would like to change - Comparing families	- Two people describe how they have changed - Two people compare similarities and differences between their families - A young man describes his recent family reunion	- Identifying the topic sentence in a paragraph - Writing a paragraph about your most positive or negative quality	- "From Circle of Friends to Modern Tribe": A group of friends can function as a family
- Talking about past mistakes - Comparing reactions to a news story - Discussing what might have caused three mysterious events - Making guesses about unusual questions - Comparing opinions about a real-life unexplained event	- A man talks about a bad decision he made - Three people talk about how they dealt with their problems - Two people talk about everyday mysteries	- Brainstorming topic sentences and supporting ideas - Writing a paragraph with dos and don'ts	- "Amnesia Spoils Newlyweds' Bliss": A man loses his memory after his wedding
- Explaining why you'd like to visit a particular city - Choosing the right city for a particular purpose - Deciding which city is best to live in - Describing your hometown - Discussing quality-of-life issues	- A TV show introduces two exciting cities - Two foreign students explain what they like about their host city - Two Sydney residents talk about the city	- Organizing ideas with a mind map - Writing a paragraph about a place you know	- "Rivals with a Lot in Common": The rivalry between two major Australian cities
- Discussing personal energy levels - Talking about how to deal with stress - Giving advice on sleep and energy levels - Talking about sleeping habits - Interpreting dreams	- Three people describe methods they use to lower stress - Two people describe their dreams and try to interpret them	- Choosing the best topic sentence - Writing a paragraph giving advice on good habits	- "To Sleep or Not to Sleep?": People are sleeping fewer hours than ever before
- Discussing conversational styles - Discussing awkward social situations - Determining appropriate topics for small talk - Comparing who you confide in - Recounting an interesting conversation	- People make small talk at parties - Two people tell some interesting news	- Making an outline - Writing about a cultural rule	- "Cell Phone Personality Types": What kind of cell phone user are you?
- Determining if a story is true or false - Presenting a recent news story - Discussing how you follow the news - Telling stories about uncomfortable situations	- A radio news broadcast - Two people describe complicated experiences - An actor describes some embarrassing moments	- Putting events in chronological order - Writing a narrative paragraph	- "It Happened to Me!": Two comical personal anecdotes

	FUNCTIONS	GRAMMAR	VOCABULARY
UNIT 7 The information age pages 54–61			
A A weird, wired world B Information overload	■ Talking about trends ■ Participating in a debate ■ Giving opinions	■ Passive of present continuous, present perfect, future ■ Negative and tag questions for giving opinions	■ Technology buzzwords ■ Expressions for connecting ideas formally ■ Words for forms of communication
UNIT 8 Putting the mind to work pages 62–69			
A Exploring creativity B Ideas that work	■ Describing job qualifications ■ Offering solutions to problems ■ Commenting on facts ■ Analyzing reasons	■ Reduced relative clauses ■ Non-defining relative clauses as sentence modifiers	■ Qualities of creative people ■ Collocations for problem solving
UNIT 9 Generally speaking pages 70–77			
A How typical are you? B Problems and solutions	■ Comparing customs and habits ■ Presenting contrasting information ■ Making generalizations ■ Talking about past habits	■ Clauses and phrases showing contrast and exception ■ Past habitual with *used to* and *would*	■ Expressions related to accepting or changing things ■ Expressions with *keep* and *stay*
UNITS 7–9 Communication review pages 78–79			
UNIT 10 The art of complaining pages 80–87			
A That really bugs me! B Let's do something about it!	■ Describing everyday annoyances ■ Describing complaining styles ■ Making and responding to complaints ■ Identifying ways to avoid problems ■ Discussing advice	■ Relative clauses and noun clauses ■ Simple and complex indirect questions	■ Expressions with *drive*, *get*, and *make* ■ *-ed* words that describe feelings
UNIT 11 Values pages 88–95			
A How honest are you? B Taking stock	■ Discussing hypothetical situations ■ Talking about values ■ Expressing wishes and regrets	■ Present unreal conditional with *unless*, *only if*, and *even if* ■ Wishes and regrets	■ Forming antonyms with prefixes ■ Adjectives that describe ethics and attitudes ■ Adjectives and nouns referring to personal values
UNIT 12 Moving around pages 96–103			
A Culture shock B Traveler or tourist?	■ Predicting the future ■ Comparing and contrasting customs ■ Making hypotheses ■ Giving advice ■ Describing preferences	■ Future perfect and future perfect continuous ■ Mixed conditionals	■ Expressions ending with prepositions ■ Compound adjectives
UNITS 10–12 Communication review pages 104–105			
GRAMMAR PLUS: Additional grammar practice and explanation pages 106–129			
VOCABULARY PLUS: Additional vocabulary practice pages 130–141			

SPEAKING	LISTENING	WRITING	READING
- Talking about Internet trends - Debating whether social networking is a positive or negative influence - Giving opinions on modern information technology - Discussing potential future technologies	- Three people talk about social networking - A news report describes health problems caused by technology	- Writing a product or service review	- "Can you spare a dime for my Gucci bills?": A woman uses the Internet to get money to pay off a frivolous debt
- Discussing jobs that require creativity - Taking a creativity quiz - Suggesting new uses for everyday items - Talking about creative thinking habits - Choosing the inventions that have had the greatest impact on modern life - Explaining why new products are invented	- Three employees explain how their jobs are creative - Two descriptions of important business and product ideas	- Choosing when to begin a new paragraph - Writing a composition about a creative or unique person	- "The Man Who Taught the World to Sing": A profile of the man who invented karaoke
- Talking about what is typical - Discussing what makes you typical or not - Discussing the effect of major life changes - Giving advice in a role play	- Three people discuss how they're unique or typical - Three people describe how they solved a problem	- Identifying supporting statements - Writing a paragraph with supporting statements	- "Painting and Problem Solving: Four Lessons": How problem solving and the dynamics of painting are alike
- Discussing how to handle irritating situations - Comparing styles of complaining - Role-playing complaints - Describing how difficult situations make you feel - Stating consumer complaints	- Two people describe irritating situations - A man uses an automated phone menu	- Writing a message of complaint	- "Dave Carroll Airs a Complaint": A musician posts music videos to complain about an airline
- Discussing the results of a survey on ethical behavior - Comparing what you would do about different ethical dilemmas - Discussing your experiences with unreliable people or services - Talking about values that are important to you - Explaining what you'd choose if you were given three wishes	- Two people describe being confronted by an ethical dilemma - Three people talk about the values that are most important to them	- Writing a thesis statement - Writing a four-paragraph composition about a happy memory or a regret	- "New York Honors a Hero": How a construction worker became a hero
- Describing the benefits and challenges of living abroad - Comparing customs between Canada and your country - Sharing bad travel experiences - Planning a trip with your group	- Three people talk about their experiences living abroad - Two people describe travel mishaps	- Writing conclusions - Writing a composition about living or traveling abroad	- "Get Yourself Lost": The best way to experience a foreign destination

1 FRIENDS AND FAMILY

LESSON A ▶ What kind of person are you?

1 STARTING POINT
Personality survey

A Do you agree with these statements? Complete the survey.

Personality Survey	Definitely agree	Somewhat agree	Definitely disagree
1. I'm not afraid of giving speeches in front of the class.	☐	☐	☐
2. I enjoy going to parties where I don't know everyone.	☐	☐	☐
3. I avoid expressing my feelings and ideas in public.	☐	☐	☐
4. I insist on making my own decisions.	☐	☐	☐
5. I don't mind giving up my time to help other people.	☐	☐	☐
6. I never worry about getting places on time.	☐	☐	☐
7. I always feel like going dancing!	☐	☐	☐
8. I can't stand being in a messy, disorganized room.	☐	☐	☐
9. I prefer telling people how I feel, even if it's embarrassing.	☐	☐	☐

B **Pair work** Compare your responses to the survey. Find two ways you and your partner are different.

"I'm not afraid of giving speeches in front of the class. How about you?"
"Oh, I'm definitely afraid of doing that!"

2 VOCABULARY & SPEAKING
How would you describe yourself?

A Which statement from the survey best matches these personality traits? Write the correct number. Then compare answers with a partner.

_2_ a. friendly and outgoing   ____ d. kind and generous   ____ g. wild and crazy
____ b. strong and independent   ____ e. honest and sincere   ____ h. calm and cool
____ c. laid-back and relaxed   ____ f. shy and reserved   ____ i. neat and tidy

B **Pair work** Choose another partner. Find two traits you have in common. Find one way that you're different.

"So, how would you describe yourself?"
"Well, I'd say I'm pretty laid-back and relaxed."
"Me, too. I never worry about getting places on time."
"I don't either. I like taking it easy and . . ."

Useful expressions	
Same traits	**Different traits**
So am I. (I am, too.)	I'm not like that.
I'm the same way.	I'd say I'm more . . .
So do I. (I do, too.)	Really? I don't.
Neither do I. (I don't either.)	That's not true for me.

VOCABULARY PLUS see page 130

3 GRAMMAR

Verbs followed by gerunds

Use the gerund form after these verbs.
I **enjoy going** to parties where I don't know everyone.
I **avoid expressing** my feelings and ideas in public.
I **don't mind giving up** my time to help other people.

Use the gerund or infinitive form after these verbs.
I **can't stand being / to be** in a messy room.
I **love taking / to take** my friends to cool new clubs.
I **hate getting up / to get up** for early morning classes.

Use the gerund form after these expressions containing prepositions.
I **insist on making** my own decisions.
I always **feel like going** dancing!
I'm **into going out** to new foreign restaurants.

GRAMMAR PLUS see page 106

A Look at the Starting Point on page 2 again. Can you find other expressions that are followed by gerunds? Which of them can also be followed by infinitives?

B Pair work How do you feel about these things? Discuss your answers using verbs or expressions followed by gerunds and infinitives.

1. tell people that I'm angry with them
2. help with chores around the house
3. listen to people's personal problems
4. eat a full meal late at night
5. start conversations with people I don't know
6. go to places where I have to use English

"I usually avoid telling people that I'm angry with them. I guess I'm just afraid of making them angry at me."

4 SPEAKING

Personal profiles

A Look at the information about these people. Which person is most similar to you? Why?

«««« Meet Your Neighbors ««««««««««

	Emily	Carlos	Linda	Chris
Job	college student	artist	lawyer	teacher
Personality	friendly and outgoing	wild and crazy	shy and reserved	laid-back and relaxed
Lifestyle	• loves playing sports • into traveling	• loves to dance • can't stand going home early	• into watching old movies	• enjoys cooking meals for friends • loves to tell jokes

B Class activity Write a similar profile for yourself. Don't write your name. Your teacher will take your profile and give you the profile of another student. Ask questions around the class to find the other student.

LESSON A What kind of person are you?

5 LISTENING
Changes

A Listen to Marcos and Heather talk about how they have changed over the last five years. How did they change? Complete the chart with the expressions from the box.

| kind and generous | friendly and outgoing | shy and reserved | wild and crazy |

	used to be . . .	has become . . .
Marcos		
Heather		

B Listen again. Choose the person you think would be more likely to do each of these things this weekend.

	Marcos	Heather
1. stay out late at a big party	☐	☐
2. stay at home and watch TV	☐	☐
3. help someone with a personal problem	☐	☐
4. invite a friend to a funny movie	☐	☐

6 DISCUSSION
How have you changed?

A How have you changed over the last five years? What do you want to change now? Complete the chart.

	How I've changed	How I'd like to change
Habits		
Personality		
Likes and dislikes		

B Pair work Compare your charts. Ask follow-up questions.

"I used to watch a lot of TV, but now I don't."
"Really? What made you change?"
"Well, I was afraid of getting out of shape. So I . . ."

Useful expressions

Describing how you've changed	Describing how you'd like to change
I used to . . . , but now I . . .	I'd like to be more . . .
I think I've become more . . .	I'm interested in . . .

UNIT 1 Friends and family

7 WRITING
Topic sentences

> The main idea is usually found in the first sentence of the paragraph. This sentence is called the topic sentence.

A Read these paragraphs about people's best and worst qualities. Underline the topic sentence in each paragraph.

I think that my most positive quality is that I'm always pretty calm and cool, especially when something breaks. I'm really into solving tricky problems and finding solutions to things. My specialty is electronics. People come to me if something goes wrong with their computers or phones. For example, two days ago, my dad's brand new tablet suddenly froze up. He was afraid of causing more damage, so he asked me to figure out the problem. It only took me 15 minutes to fix it, and I loved doing it!

My most negative quality is that I'm not very neat and tidy. Sometimes I worry about being so disorganized, but I never feel like doing anything about it. My apartment is always a mess, so I can never find anything. Last week, for example, I finished doing some homework and then started to make dinner. In the morning, I couldn't find my assignment anywhere, so I had to redo it. I really want to change my bad habits, but I don't know where to start.

B Think about your own personal qualities. Make a list. Then decide which quality is the most positive and which is the most negative. Circle each one.

C Write a paragraph about either your most positive or your most negative quality. Make sure your paragraph has only one main idea.

D **Pair work** Exchange paragraphs with a partner. Then answer the questions.
1. What is your partner's topic sentence? Underline it.
2. What examples does your partner give to support the topic sentence?
3. What do you find most interesting about your partner's paragraph?

LESSON B ▶ Every family is different.

1 STARTING POINT
Different types of families

A Look at the families in the pictures. What's different about each type of family?

What's Your Family Like?

The Wangs, Vancouver
"We're an **extended family** now that Grandma has moved in. The big advantage of having her at home is that she can babysit more often."

The Watsons, Sydney
"My wife and I both work now, and the extra money is great. The only trouble with being a **two-income family** is we don't spend as much time together."

The Patels, London
"We're a typical **nuclear family** – it's just my sister, my parents, and me. The only bad thing about living in our house is there's only one bathroom!"

B Pair work What are some more advantages and disadvantages of each type of family in part A? Compare ideas.

"In a nuclear family, you might not see your grandparents every day. That's a disadvantage."

2 LISTENING & SPEAKING
How are their families different?

A Listen to Paul and Andrea talk about their families. What kind of family did each person grow up in? How have their families changed?

B Listen again. Match the people on the left with the phrases on the right.

1. Andrea _b_
2. Andrea's husband ___
3. Andrea's sister-in-law ___
4. Paul's sister ___
5. Paul ___
6. Paul's mother ___

a. has two daughters.
b. doesn't know her in-laws very well.
c. has three brothers.
d. is looking forward to seeing the family.
e. will be cooking for 12 people.
f. is a law student.

C Pair work Is your family similar to Paul's or Andrea's? How is it similar? How is it different?

6 UNIT 1 Friends and family

3 GRAMMAR

Noun clauses after *be*

A noun clause is a part of a sentence with a subject and a predicate that functions as a noun. *That* is optional in noun clauses after *be*. Also notice the prepositions followed by gerunds in the first part of the sentences.

The only trouble **with** being a two-income family is **(that) we don't spend as much time together**.
The big advantage **of** having Grandma at home is **(that) she can babysit more often**.

GRAMMAR PLUS see page 107

A Look at the Starting Point on page 6 again. Can you find the noun clause in the last paragraph? Which preposition is used in the first part of the sentence?

B Combine the sentences. Then compare answers with a partner.

1. I'm the youngest in the family. The nice thing is I get a lot of attention.
   The nice thing about being the youngest in the family is that I get a lot of attention.
2. I have a younger sister. The trouble is she always wants to borrow my clothes.
3. I'm away at college. The bad part is that I miss my family.
4. I work at night. The worst thing is I can't have dinner with my family.
5. I'm the oldest in the family. One bad thing is that I always have to babysit.

C Complete the sentences with your own ideas. Then compare answers with a partner.

1. An advantage of being a twin is . . .
   that you always have someone to hang out with.
2. A problem with being an only child is . . .
3. One benefit of being the oldest is . . .
4. A big disadvantage of having an older sibling is . . .
5. The best thing about having a big family is . . .

4 DISCUSSION

Family matters

A Choose at least three questions you'd like to talk about with your group.

- ☐ What's the best thing about spending time with your family? What's the worst thing?
- ☐ What's one advantage of having a close family?
- ☐ What are some rules that people have to follow in your family?
- ☐ What's a benefit of having strict parents?
- ☐ Are you most likely to confide in a parent, a sibling, or a friend?
- ☐ Do you believe mothers and fathers should do the same chores?
- ☐ What are the advantages and disadvantages of having a two-income family?

B **Group work** Discuss the questions you chose in part A. Ask follow-up questions and make sure everyone in your group participates.

5 VOCABULARY
Compound family terms

A Match the family members on the left with the definitions on the right.

1. Your great-aunt is ____
2. Your granddaughter is ____
3. Your sister-in-law is ____
4. Your great-grandmother is ____

a. your father's or mother's grandmother.
b. your mother's or father's aunt.
c. your son's or daughter's daughter.
d. your wife's or husband's sister, or your brother's wife.

B **Pair work** Which of the family members in the box can be combined with a prefix or suffix in the chart? Complete the chart with a partner. What does each term mean?

| aunt | daughter | mother | niece | son |
| brother | father | nephew | sister | uncle |

great-	grand-	great-grand-	-in-law
aunt	daughter	mother	sister

"Your great-nephew is your brother's or sister's grandson."

VOCABULARY PLUS see page 130

6 LISTENING
Family reunion

A Listen to Victor tell a friend about his family reunion. What were they celebrating at the reunion?

B Listen again. In addition to Victor, who else was at the reunion? Select the people mentioned.

☐ 1. his grandfather ☐ 4. his sister-in-law ☐ 7. his mother-in-law
☐ 2. his uncle's cousin ☐ 5. his niece ☐ 8. his cousin
☐ 3. his brother ☐ 6. his son ☐ 9. friends of the family

7 READING
A family of friends

A **Group work** Do you tend to rely more on friends or family for help and advice? Why? Discuss with your group.

From Circle of Friends to Modern Tribe

Who celebrates birthdays and holidays with you? Who do you call when a crisis hits or when good luck strikes? If your answer is "my friends," you may have a "tribe."

When Ethan Watters took stock of his life a few years ago, the San Francisco writer realized that he was more dependent on friends than family, who lived hundreds of miles away.

"My friends were the centerpiece of my social life," he says. "They had taken on all the responsibilities that family members typically tackle – connecting me to the city, being a matchmaker, and helping me find jobs and places to live."

This circle of friends had become a tribe, which started when a group of artists, writers, and photographers began meeting for dinner every Tuesday night. Before long, they had begun functioning as a family of choice.

Watters grew to believe that non-family members forming close-knit social networks was a growing trend in the United States, and he wrote a book about it called *Urban Tribes: Are Friends the New Family?*

Modern tribes like Watters's often grow out of a shared interest or experience, but not every group of friends becomes a tribe.

The shift from "circle of friends" to tribe happens when members begin to treat each other like family – offering support without expectation of repayment; sheltering each other from gossip, stress, and attack; and looking out for everyone's overall well-being in life, work, and relationships.

Modern tribes often have a regular meeting place, annual parties, and group trips. Shared rites and rituals create a tribal story. "The members of the group may change," Watters says, "but the story of that group has central elements that remain. It gives the group a history."

Every tribe usually has an individual or core group that tends to its growth and survival. These tribal leaders are the ones who get everyone together on a regular basis and make the phone calls that get members excited about upcoming events.

Like families, tribes have a way of shaping their members: Individuals feel more confident, secure, loved, and stable. Even if your own family is close-knit, you may benefit from cultivating a family-like circle of friends. "The love and support we get from one," Watters says, "does not take away from the love and support we get from another."

Source: "My Tribe," by Erin Peterson, Experience Life

B Read the article and answer the questions. Then compare answers with a partner.

1. In what ways does Watters's circle of friends function as a family?
2. According to the article, what are some differences between a tribe and a family?
3. How does a group of friends become a tribe?

C **Group work** Discuss these questions. Then share your answers with the class.

1. What are some advantages and disadvantages of relying on friends for family-like support?
2. Do you consider yourself a member of a modern tribe? Why or why not?

2 MISTAKES AND MYSTERIES
LESSON A ▶ Life lessons

1 STARTING POINT
Learning the hard way

A Read about these people's problems. What mistake did each person make?

What Did I Get Myself Into?
Three mistakes that led to big messes

I was supposed to be studying for a math test this weekend, but my friends made me go to the beach with them instead. I mean, I didn't have to go with them, but I did. Now the test is in two hours, and I'm totally unprepared. I should have stayed home and studied!
— **Alicia, Tepic, Mexico**

In high school, I had to wear a uniform, so I didn't have a lot of fashionable clothes. When I started college, I thought I needed to have more, so I wasted a lot of money on trendy outfits. But I really shouldn't have done it. Now I'm broke!
— **Kenichi, Osaka, Japan**

We weren't supposed to cook in our dorm rooms, but I had a microwave anyway. The cafeteria was right next door, so I really didn't need to have it. Anyway, I got caught making popcorn last week, and the school took the microwave away.
— **Melanie, Toronto, Canada**

B Pair work What should each person do differently in the future? Compare ideas.

"I don't think Alicia should listen to her friends in the future."
"Yeah, I agree. She shouldn't let them influence her like that."

2 LISTENING
I'll never do that again!

🔊 **A** Listen to Frank talk about a bad decision he made. What was his decision? Why was it a bad one?

🔊 **B** Listen again. Are these statements true or false? Choose the correct answer.

	True	False
1. Frank and his neighbor were good friends.	☐	☐
2. Frank knew he was allergic to cats.	☐	☐
3. Frank marked his calendar to remember to feed the cat.	☐	☐
4. Frank forgot what time his train was going to leave.	☐	☐
5. Frank remembered to feed the cat on Saturday.	☐	☐

3 GRAMMAR

Past modals and phrasal modals of obligation

Should have, *was supposed to*, *had to*, and *needed to* all describe obligations in the past, although they have slightly different uses.

I **should have** stayed home and studied! *(It was a good idea, but I didn't do it.)*
I **was supposed to** be studying this weekend. *(It was expected, but I didn't do it.)*
I **had to** wear a uniform. *(We were forced to do this.)*
I **didn't have to** go with my friends, but I did. *(There was no obligation.)*
I thought I **needed to** have more clothes. *(I thought this was necessary.)*

GRAMMAR PLUS *see page 108*

A Look at the Starting Point on page 10 again. Can you find other examples of past modals and phrasal modals of obligation? What does each one mean?

B Choose the answer that is true for each sentence. Then compare answers with a partner.

1. I shouldn't have invited them.
   - ☐ a. I didn't invite them.
   - ☐ b. I invited them.

2. That was a secret! You weren't supposed to tell anyone!
   - ☐ a. You didn't tell anyone.
   - ☐ b. You told someone.

3. We didn't have to study for the test.
   - ☐ a. We forgot to study.
   - ☐ b. We were prepared for the test.

4. I know Jane didn't like my cooking, but she didn't need to be so rude about it.
   - ☐ a. Jane was rude to me.
   - ☐ b. Jane wasn't rude to me.

C Complete the sentences with information about yourself. Then compare answers with a partner.

1. After I started high school, I had to . . .
   study a lot harder.
2. I made someone angry once because I wasn't supposed to . . .
3. I wasted a lot of money once because I thought I needed to . . .
4. When I had the opportunity, I should have . . .

4 DISCUSSION

Past experiences

A Look at the survey and choose the items that are true for you.

Have you ever . . .
- ☐ enjoyed doing something you weren't supposed to do?
- ☐ not done something you should have done?
- ☐ done something foolish that you didn't need to do?
- ☐ had to follow a rule you didn't like?
- ☐ had to enforce a rule you didn't like?

B Pair work Discuss your answers. Ask follow-up questions.

"Have you ever enjoyed doing something you weren't supposed to do?"
"Sure. At my old job, I wasn't supposed to take a long lunch, but I took long lunches at the park, anyway. How about you?"

LESSON A Life lessons

5 VOCABULARY
Recognizing problems

A These verbs are often used to talk about problems. Use the verbs to replace the boldfaced words and phrases in the sentences.

aggravate	
avoid	
cause	
deal with	a problem
identify	
ignore	
run into	
solve	

1. My friend **never does anything about** his problems.
   My friend always ignores his problems.
2. Maria can look at a broken bicycle and **find** the problem right away.
3. My sister is never afraid to **try to take care of** a difficult problem.
4. Dan always **makes** his problems **worse**.
5. Ruby always follows the recipe closely to **prevent** problems when she cooks.
6. Michael always **unexpectedly encounters** problems when he tries to fix things.
7. Carla is great at **completely fixing** any kind of problem at work.
8. Al is the kind of student who always **makes** problems for teachers.

B Pair work Tell your partner about people you know who are similar to the people in the sentences in part A.

"My cousin always ignores her problems. Her car is always making strange noises, but she never does anything about it."

VOCABULARY PLUS see page 131

6 LISTENING
Dealing with problems

A Listen to Ray (*R*), Felipe (*F*), and Jennifer (*J*) talk about a problem that they each had. What did each person finally do about the problem? Write the correct letter.

____ ignored it   ____ dealt with it   ____ aggravated it

B Listen again. Briefly describe each person's problem.

Ray: _____
Felipe: _____
Jennifer: _____

UNIT 2 Mistakes and mysteries

7 WRITING
Brainstorming

Brainstorming means making a list of ideas about a topic. Then you can use this list to come up with a topic sentence and ideas to support it.

A Group work Brainstorm as many ideas as you can to add to the dos and don'ts for living on a budget.

Living on a Tight Budget

Do	Don't
• compare prices	• buy the first thing you see
• look for sales	• buy brand names
• check ads for used items	• use credit cards

B Group work Brainstorm dos and don'ts for one of these topics. Write your ideas.

- getting over a bad cold
- staying safe in a big city
- preparing for entrance exams

C Read this paragraph about living on a tight budget. Then write a topic sentence and a similar paragraph about your topic using your ideas.

> Living on a tight budget is easy if you follow some simple rules when you go shopping. First of all, you should never buy something at the first store you visit. You need to check at least a few other stores and go online to compare prices. Second, don't be in a hurry! If you take your time, you might find a sale. If there are no sales right now, ask a salesperson if there's going to be one soon. Third, consider buying used, or secondhand, items. You can check in the newspaper or online to find what you're looking for. Finally, you might get a better price at some stores by paying cash instead of using a credit card, so be sure to ask about cash discounts.

D Pair work Exchange brainstorming lists and paragraphs with a partner. Then answer the questions.

1. How many brainstorming ideas did your partner use? Do you think he or she chose the best ones?
2. Do you have any questions about your partner's paragraph? Is there anything you disagree with?
3. Can you think of a good title for your partner's paragraph? Explain your choice.

LESSON B ▶ *I can't explain it!*

1 STARTING POINT
A mysterious artist

A Read the article and the comments on the right. Whose comments do you agree with?

The Mystery of BANKSY

Banksy is a British graffiti artist who has become famous around the world for two things: his controversial work and the mystery surrounding him. Usually working in disguise or at night, Banksy has managed to keep his identity secret and both his fans and detractors alert. Any clues to his identity always make the news.

In 2010, *Time* magazine featured Banksy as one of the 100 most influential people of the year. Readers hoping to finally see his face must have been pretty disappointed when they saw the picture of Banksy – with a paper bag over his head.

In 2011, when a movie by Banksy was nominated for an Oscar, his graffiti appeared on buildings and signs around Los Angeles. (People thought he could have been trying to get publicity for the movie.) At that time, a passerby photographed a man busy taking photos of the graffiti. It may have been Banksy documenting his own work, but nobody is sure.

In 2013, a website claimed Banksy had been arrested and his identity finally revealed. However, the claims were later discovered to be false. It's not clear who was behind the hoax, but one thing was certain: Banksy's secret was still safe.

Reader Comments

CafeLife: People should stop trying to find out who Banksy is. It's a waste of time.

Hye_Jung: The magazine readers shouldn't have expected Banksy to reveal his identity just because of an article.

Paul2001: I'm certain Banksy must have wanted to win that Oscar. But would he have shown his face at the award ceremony?

ArtFan: Banksy does return to photograph his art, so it might have been him taking the pictures. He should be more careful.

Zorro565: Banksy shouldn't have painted on other people's property. That's illegal.

WebWatcher: That website hoax might have been planned by Banksy himself. What a joke.

More >>

B **Pair work** Compare your reactions to the article.

"The people who worked on his movie might know who Banksy is."
"Well, maybe, but I'm sure his family must know he is the mysterious artist."

2 GRAMMAR

Modals with multiple uses

To express degrees of certainty, use *must (not)*, *can't*, *could (not)*, *might (not)*, or *may (not)*.
I'm certain Banksy **must have wanted** to win that Oscar.
People thought he **could have been trying** to get publicity for the movie.
That website hoax **might have been planned** by Banksy himself.

To express obligation, advice, or opinions, use *should (not)*. Do not use *must (not) have* for obligations, advice, or opinions about the past.
Banksy **shouldn't have painted** on other people's property. *(obligation)*
He **should be** more careful. *(advice)*
The magazine readers **shouldn't have expected** Banksy to reveal his identity just because of an article. *(opinion)*

Also notice how these modals are used in the passive and continuous.

GRAMMAR PLUS see page 109

A Look at the Starting Point on page 14 again. What does each modal express? Which one is used in the passive?

B Use modals to write reactions to these situations. Then compare answers with a partner.

1. You and your friend planned to meet, but your friend never arrived.
   He might have been busy at work, but he should have called to tell me.
2. You loaned your classmate a lot of money last week, but she still hasn't repaid you.
3. You feel sick after a big fish dinner.
4. You receive flowers from a secret admirer.
5. You haven't received any phone calls or text messages in a week.
6. Your boss promised to promote you, but it still hasn't happened.

3 DISCUSSION

What's the explanation?

A Read these headlines about strange events. How would you explain them?

MYSTERY SOUND IRRITATES VILLAGE
Each night from midnight to 4 A.M., a mysterious humming sound keeps the 300 residents of Woodland, England, awake. There are no factories or large roads nearby, and so far nobody can explain the sound.

Colored Honey Puzzles Farmers
In a French region famous for its honey, bees have been producing it in shades of blue and green. Farmers say the honey is unsellable, and they are investigating the cause.

River Runs Red
Shocked residents watched in disbelief last week as the river running through their city turned a deep red color. Some people rushed to save a bottle of the colored water while they had the chance.

B **Group work** Discuss your explanations. Do you agree?

"Airplanes flying overhead could have caused the noise in that village."
"I'm not so sure. I think someone may have been making the sound on purpose as a prank."

Useful expressions

Disagreeing
I don't know.
I'm not so sure.
Well, maybe, but . . .
I know what you mean, but . . .

LESSON B I can't explain it!

4 VOCABULARY & SPEAKING
Verbs of belief

A Put these verbs of belief in the correct columns. Discuss your answers with a partner.

| assume | be positive | bet | figure | have a hunch | suppose |
| be certain | be sure | doubt | guess | know for a fact | suspect |

Certain	Not certain
	assume

B Group work Use the verbs of belief to discuss these questions.

1. Why do giraffes have long necks?
2. Why do some buildings not have a thirteenth floor?
3. Is there life on other planets?
4. Why doesn't a haircut hurt?
5. Why do some people fall in love at first sight?
6. What color is an insect's blood?

"Why do giraffes have long necks?"
"I'm not sure, but I assume they have long necks to eat the leaves at the tops of trees."
"Yeah, I bet that's the reason why."

VOCABULARY PLUS see page 131

5 LISTENING & SPEAKING
Solving mysteries

A Listen to Sheila and Adam discussing some myths and mysteries researched by the TV show *Solving Mysteries*. Choose the ones discovered to be true.

☐ 1. Using a cell phone can cause a fire at a gas station.
☐ 2. Talking to plants for a short time will help them grow better.
☐ 3. A person can break a glass using just his or her voice.
☐ 4. Yawning is contagious.

B Listen again. What ideas did Sheila and Adam originally have? Answer the questions.

1. How did Sheila think that cell phones could cause fires?
   _____

2. Why did Adam doubt that talking to plants could help them grow?
   _____

3. Why did Sheila have trouble believing voices could break a glass?
   _____

4. Why didn't Adam believe that yawning could be contagious?
   _____

C Group work Brainstorm other mysteries you might like to have *Solving Mysteries* investigate for you. Can anyone in the group explain the mysteries?

6 READING
Do I know you?

A Group work What does *amnesia* mean? What are some things that might cause amnesia? Discuss with your group.

Amnesia Spoils Newlyweds' Bliss

What if the person you married forgot who you were? For one Texas couple, marriage became a blind date when the groom came down with amnesia days after their wedding.

Amy and Sean McNulty's wedding day started well, but ended with a shock. One of Sean's good friends was in a serious car accident after the wedding and ended up in a coma. Nevertheless, Amy and Sean decided to make their honeymoon trip according to plans.

At the airport, Sean realized he'd left his wallet in their car. He said to Amy, "I'll be right back." But he didn't return.

Amy contacted the police, who found Sean wandering near a motel three days later. He was confused and covered in bug bites. He had no idea who he was or who Amy was. Sean could not remember any personal details from his life, not even his mother.

Amy was now married to a man who viewed her as a stranger. "I wondered, you know, is he going to remember me? How is our relationship going to, you know, form?" said Amy. This was a big change after a six-year courtship and plenty of shared memories.

When Sean got out of the hospital, Amy had to give him a tour of their home. Although he had a room devoted to music, he couldn't even remember what it meant to hear music.

Psychiatrist Dr. Daniel Brown says Sean's amnesia might have been caused by a series of stressful moments, like his friend's car accident. According to Dr. Brown, Sean's brain didn't connect with his identity anymore. "He doesn't know who Sean McNulty is and has no personal memories or autobiographical memories to account for who he might be."

Dr. Brown explained that amnesia was like forgetting the name of a file you stored on your computer. "You know it's there but you can't find it," said Brown. "His memory is like that. He still has the file."

Fortunately, better times soon arrived. The day before their first anniversary, Sean's memories flooded back in an instant. He soon remembered everything, including their wedding. "I remember shoving cake in her face," said Sean. "It was great."

Sean views the experience as a chance to confirm he picked the right bride. "I got to see how much she loves me," said Sean. "We have a much stronger and closer bond from the experience. I couldn't have found a better woman to spend my life with."

Source: "Amnesia Spoils Newlyweds' Bliss," *ABC News*

B Read the article. Are these statements true or false? Choose the correct answer.

	True	False
1. Sean's amnesia began after he was in a car accident.	☐	☐
2. Sean and Amy didn't know each other well before they got married.	☐	☐
3. Sean shoved cake in Amy's face when he remembered who she was.	☐	☐
4. The amnesia might have been caused by stress.	☐	☐

C Group work Discuss these questions. Then share your answers with the class.

1. What would you have done if you had been in Amy's position?
2. What would be some of the problems you'd face if you ever forgot everything?

LESSON B I can't explain it!

3 EXPLORING NEW CITIES

LESSON A ▶ Popular destinations

1 STARTING POINT
Cities of the world

A Read about these cities. Which city would you most like to visit?

BARCELONA

Barcelona is famous for museums, nightlife, and seafood – and for the architect Antoni Gaudí, who designed several of the city's most distinctive buildings. Most restaurants here stay open until midnight, when many locals are still enjoying dinner.

BEIJING

Beijing has many popular tourist attractions, which include the Summer Palace and the Forbidden City. Tourists who come here for the first time are amazed by the crowds, the busy streets, and the constantly changing skyline.

SEOUL

Seoul is well known for its spicy food and its shopping areas, where you can find everything from antique pottery to custom-made clothing. The Myeong-dong area has dozens of shops that sell the latest fashions.

SYDNEY

The place where most tourists go first in Sydney is the famous Opera House, but this Australian city also has great restaurants and museums. The spring and fall are the seasons when most people come to visit.

B Pair work Tell your partner about a city you know.

"I know Vancouver. It's got the ocean on one side and mountains on the other. It's really beautiful, but it's expensive . . ."

2 LISTENING
Where in the world . . . ?

🔊 **A** Listen to Diana and Matt talk about two cities. Who is talking about Athens and who is talking about Seoul?

🔊 **B** Listen again. Who mentions these topics, Diana (*D*) or Matt (*M*)? Write the correct letter.

____ 1. founded 3,000 years ago   ____ 4. a river   ____ 7. traffic
____ 2. delicious spicy food   ____ 5. a subway system   ____ 8. street vendors
____ 3. beautiful beaches   ____ 6. monuments   ____ 9. nightlife

3 GRAMMAR

Defining and non-defining relative clauses

A defining relative clause defines or gives essential information about a noun.
The Myeong-dong area has dozens of shops **that sell the latest fashions**.
The spring and fall are the seasons **when most people come to visit**.

A non-defining relative clause gives optional information about a noun and cannot begin with the pronoun *that*. Notice the use of commas.
Most restaurants here stay open until midnight, **when many locals are still enjoying dinner**.
Beijing has many popular tourist attractions, **which include the Summer Palace and the Forbidden City**.

GRAMMAR PLUS see page 110

A Look at the Starting Point on page 18 again. Can you find more relative clauses?

B Underline the relative clauses in the sentences and add commas where necessary. Write *D* for a defining and *ND* for a non-defining relative clause.

ND 1. Bangkok, which is the capital of Thailand, has many excellent restaurants and markets.
___ 2. Over one million people come to Pamplona in July when the festival of San Fermín takes place in this Spanish city.
___ 3. Aden is an ancient port city that is located in southern Yemen.
___ 4. Bogotá which is situated on a high plateau in central Colombia has frequently changing weather.
___ 5. Montreal is a sophisticated city where some of the best cuisine in Canada is found.
___ 6. São Paulo which is the biggest city in Brazil is one of the world's most populated cities.

C Join the sentences using non-defining relative clauses. Then compare answers.

1. Gaudí designed Barcelona's Park Güell. You can see fabulous sculptures there.
2. Seoul's name comes from the ancient word *seorabeol*. *Seorabeol* means "capital."
3. The center of Beijing is Tiananmen Square. It is the world's largest public square.
4. A great time to visit Seoul is in the fall. This is when Koreans celebrate the Chuseok festival.
5. Fast-food restaurants are already fairly common in China. They are increasing in number each year.
6. Australia's first European settlers came to Sydney in the late 1700s. They were originally from Great Britain.

4 SPEAKING

A great place to visit

A Which of the cities on page 18 would you like to visit? Write three sentences explaining your reasons. Use relative clauses where appropriate.

Barcelona is a city that I'd like to visit because . . .

B **Pair work** Tell your partner which city you'd like to visit and why.

LESSON A Popular destinations

5 VOCABULARY
What makes a city?

A Are these features of cities more important to tourists or to residents? Put the words in the correct columns. Add ideas of your own.

| climate | crime rate | green spaces | job market | neighborhoods | shopping |
| cost of living | cuisine | hotels | landmarks | nightlife | transportation system |

Important to tourists	Important to residents	Important to both

B Pair work Use the features from part A to talk about your city. Give examples and add extra information.

"Salvador is famous all over Brazil for its cuisine. Acarajé is one of the most popular foods, and it's really delicious. It's a deep-fried cake that's made from mashed beans."

VOCABULARY PLUS see page 132

6 LISTENING
What's the city like?

A Listen to Carlos and Vicki talk about San Francisco. Who seems to like the city better?

B Listen again. Choose the city features that Carlos and Vicki mention.

☐ 1. climate ☐ 3. shopping ☐ 5. hotels ☐ 7. landmarks ☐ 9. cuisine
☐ 2. architecture ☐ 4. customs ☐ 6. job market ☐ 8. nightlife

7 DISCUSSION
Perfect places

A Answer the questions with your own ideas.

What is...
1. a good city for budget travelers? _____
2. a good city for a honeymoon? _____
3. a place that would make a great family vacation spot? _____
4. a city where you'd like to live for a few years? _____
5. a good city to go to school in? _____
6. a place that you would never want to visit? _____

B Pair work Discuss your answers.

"I think New York is a good place for budget travelers."

"I'm not sure I agree. New York is incredibly expensive."

"That's true, but there are lots of cheap fast-food restaurants . . ."

Useful expressions

Agreeing with an opinion	Disagreeing with an opinion
I think you're right.	I'm not sure I agree.
I'm with you.	Maybe, but don't you think . . . ?
That's true.	Really?
I think so, too.	I know what you mean, but . . .

C Group work Join another pair and try to agree on one answer for each question.

UNIT 3 Exploring new cities

8 WRITING
Organizing ideas with a mind map

> Making a mind map is a good way of organizing your brainstorming ideas. Mind maps help you map out the supporting details about your topic.

A Look at the phrases in the box about Cuzco, Peru. Choose the main idea and write it in the center of the mind map. Then write the supporting details around it.

| a mix of history and culture | great shopping | something for everyone |
| beautiful architecture | nice hotels | wonderful restaurants |

B Read the paragraph about Cuzco. Underline the ideas from the mind map in the paragraph.

<u>Cuzco has something for everyone.</u> It's one of the oldest cities in the Americas, and it was once the capital of the Inca empire. Today, Cuzco is Peru's tourist capital because of its unique mix of history and culture. People who are interested in architecture will love the nearby Inca ruins of Machu Picchu and the palace of Inca Roca. Cuzco has many places to stay, which range from first-class hotels to cozy inns. There are also many cafés and restaurants where you can eat delicious local dishes or international cuisine. Also, Cuzco has great markets where you can shop for local arts and crafts. When you visit Cuzco, you should try to experience all it has to offer.

C Choose a place you know and make your own mind map. Be sure the main idea is general and the map contains several supporting ideas.

D Write a paragraph based on the ideas in your mind map.

E **Pair work** Exchange paragraphs with a partner. Then answer the questions.

1. Are there enough supporting details? Are there any details you'd like your partner to add?
2. Does the content of the paragraph reflect the ideas in the mind map?
3. Would you like to visit the place your partner wrote about? Why or why not?

LESSON A Popular destinations

LESSON B ▶ My kind of town

1 STARTING POINT
City search

A Complete the descriptions with the sentences below. Then compare answers.

This exciting large city with bustling streets is a great place to live. Most evenings you can choose from a movie, a concert, or even a museum. (1) ____ There are lots of jobs here, and the average salary is about $4,000 per month. (2) ____ Our efficient new subway system can get you anywhere you want to go. (3) ____

This is a picturesque little resort town with year-round outdoor activities. There's something to do in all four seasons. But there's not much action here at night. (4) ____ There are many quaint little stores and boutiques in this beautiful town. (5) ____ Apartments are affordable, too. You can get a great place for about $1,000 a month, and average monthly salaries are about $2,500. (6) ____

a. However, housing costs are high. A nice apartment is about $2,500 per month.
b. So, even though our streets are safe, the evenings can be dull.
c. But be careful – in spite of all the late-night activity, the crime rate is high.
d. On the other hand, it can sometimes be difficult to find a job.
e. Although it's fast, clean, and cheap, it's pretty crowded during rush hour. Nevertheless, it's becoming one of the most popular ways for people to get to work.
f. Despite the attractive location, the prices of houses are surprisingly reasonable.

B Pair work Which place do you think has more to offer – the city or the town?

2 VOCABULARY
Compound terms for towns

A These compound terms describe different types of towns. How would you define each one?

border town	college town	mountain town	resort town	suburban town
coastal town	industrial town	port town	rural town	tourist town

A border town is near a border with another state or country.

B Pair work Which of the terms best describes your hometown? Which best describes the town where you'd like to live someday? Compare ideas.

VOCABULARY PLUS see page 132

3 GRAMMAR
Order of modifiers

When two or more modifiers occur in a sentence, they usually follow this order.

	Quality	Size	Age	Type	Noun	Descriptive phrase
this	exciting	large			city	with bustling streets
a	picturesque	little		resort	town	with year-round outdoor activities
a	run-down		old	port	town	that has seen better days

GRAMMAR PLUS see page 111

A Look at the Starting Point on page 22 again. Can you find more sentences that have two or more modifiers?

B Write descriptions of places you know. Then compare answers with a partner.

1. a nearby city or town that you frequently visit
   Middleton is a typical suburban town with a good shopping mall.
2. a place you'd like to visit one day
3. a place tourists to your country want to see
4. a place you enjoy visiting, but wouldn't want to live in

4 GRAMMAR
Connecting contrasting ideas

You can use these words and phrases to connect contrasting ideas.

despite	although	however	on the other hand
in spite of	even though	nevertheless	

GRAMMAR PLUS see page 111

A Look at the Starting Point on page 22 again. What words and phrases connect the contrasting ideas?

B Choose the words that are true for you. Then complete the sentences.

1. Although I (would) / wouldn't like to live in this town forever, . . .
   Although I would like to live in this town forever, I'll have to move if rents go up.
2. There are *not many / a lot of* things I like about this town. However, . . .
3. Even though finding an apartment is *easy / difficult* in this town, . . .
4. Despite the high cost of living in this city, there are *a number of / no* . . .
5. The *spring / summer / fall / winter* here is very nice. On the other hand, . . .
6. Most places in this town close *early / late*. In spite of that, . . .
7. The areas around this town are mainly *rural / suburban / urban*. Nevertheless, . . .

C Pair work Discuss your answers. Ask and answer follow-up questions.

"Although I'd like to live in this town forever, I'll have to move if rents go up."
"Really? Where would you move?"
"I'm not sure. I hope someplace cheaper, but still near here."

5 LISTENING
Life in Sydney

🔊 **A** Listen to Maria and Ian talk about life in Sydney. Who seems to enjoy living there more?

🔊 **B** Listen again. Which person has these opinions? Choose Maria, Ian, or both.

	Maria	Ian	Both
1. It's easy to get around Sydney.	☐	☐	☐
2. The beaches are great.	☐	☐	☐
3. The rents are expensive.	☐	☐	☐
4. It's a fun place to live.	☐	☐	☐
5. The restaurants are all expensive.	☐	☐	☐
6. Life is better in a smaller town.	☐	☐	☐

6 DISCUSSION
Quality of life

A Rate these quality-of-life issues as very important (2), important (1), or not important (0). Can you add one more to the list?

Quality of Life

____ affordable housing   ____ exciting nightlife   ____ pleasant weather

____ a variety of restaurants   ____ first-class health care   ____ varied retail shops

____ beautiful parks   ____ historic neighborhoods   ____ wireless hot spots

____ convenient public transportation   ____ low crime rates   ____ _____

B Pair work Which three issues are the most important to you personally when considering where to live? Explain why.

"I guess affordable housing and exciting nightlife are the most important to me. I'd love to find a place I could afford that was near someplace fun."

"I know what you mean. But for me, I guess low crime rates are probably the most important. I want to live somewhere where I feel safe. I don't mind if it's a little boring."

C Class activity Share your answers with your classmates. Which issues were mentioned most often?

UNIT 3 Exploring new cities

7 READING
Melbourne versus Sydney

A Pair work What do you know about the Australian cities of Melbourne and Sydney? Tell your partner. Then read the article.

RIVALS with a lot IN COMMON
What's the truth behind the rivalry between Melbourne and Sydney?

According to Melbournians, they live in a paradise where ideas are discussed, the arts are celebrated, and life is beautiful. Sydneysiders claim to live in the same kind of place – only better. Nobody can agree on how the rivalry between Sydney and Melbourne started, but it's been going on for as long as anyone can remember.

If you believe the stereotypes that fuel this rivalry, Melbourne is just a quaint coastal city with nothing to do unless you're into indie music festivals and a slow-paced lifestyle, while Sydney is an expensive, unfriendly place with a focus on business and no place to park. If you believe what Melbournians and Sydneysiders say, the cities don't have much in common except that they're both Australian cities whose residents love where they live.

In reality, Sydney is a warm, beautiful city with lots of green, cross-harbor ferries, and world-class beaches, while Melbourne's right-in-the-city beaches are near colorful neighborhoods where there are plenty of things to do for entertainment.

Both Melbourne and Sydney have fabulous restaurants featuring cuisine from just about anywhere in the world, and both offer nightlife possibilities with something for everyone. In addition, both cities feature a year-round schedule of art and music festivals, as well as other cultural events catering to every taste. And their excellent public transportation systems help you get around easily.

It's true that Melbourne tends to have less rain than Sydney and that Sydney's average temperatures are higher, but it's wonderfully pleasant in either place. And while the cost-of-living is a little lower in Melbourne and salaries are higher in Sydney, prices in both really are quite comparable.

So, what's the rivalry all about? It probably comes down to civic pride. Residents of both of these world-class cities are rightly proud of where they live, and though there are differences, the differences are not really all that extreme. If you're not convinced, visit both and see for yourself.

B Read the article again. Are these statements true (*T*), false (*F*), or is the information not given (*NG*) in the article? Write the correct letters.

____ 1. The rivalry between Sydney and Melbourne is a recent development.

____ 2. Life in Sydney, like in Melbourne, can also be slow.

____ 3. It's hard to get anywhere in Melbourne or Sydney without a car.

____ 4. It costs slightly less to live in Melbourne than it does in Sydney.

C Group work Discuss these questions. Then share your answers with the class.

1. Why do you think people in Melbourne and Sydney tend to focus on the differences between the two cities rather than on the similarities?

2. Are there any cities in your country that have a rivalry? How are the cities similar and different? Is the rivalry based on stereotypes or on facts?

COMMUNICATION REVIEW
UNITS 1–3

✓ SELF-ASSESSMENT

How well can you do these things? Choose the best answer.

I can . . .	Very well	OK	A little
▸ Express personal likes and dislikes and give relevant explanations (Ex. 1)	☐	☐	☐
▸ Make and evaluate recommendations to improve a city in a problem-solving discussion (Ex. 2)	☐	☐	☐
▸ Understand anecdotes and say how the speakers feel about past mistakes (Ex. 3)	☐	☐	☐
▸ Describe past mistakes in my life (Ex. 3)	☐	☐	☐
▸ Give a presentation about "must-see" places in my city and explain my choices (Ex. 4)	☐	☐	☐

Now do the corresponding exercises. Was your assessment correct?

1 DISCUSSION
Likes and dislikes

A Look at these items. Can you think of a personal example for each one?

1. something you're into / not into doing by yourself
2. the kind of music you feel like listening to when you're in a bad mood
3. something you like doing when you're stressed out
4. a household chore you don't mind / can't stand doing
5. something you avoid doing, if possible

B Pair work Discuss your answers with a partner.

"I'm really into going to art galleries by myself. That way I can spend as much time as I want."

"Oh, I'm just the opposite. I don't really like going to galleries alone. It's nice to share the experience with someone."

2 DISCUSSION
The people's action committee

A Pair work You are members of an action group that has been asked to suggest improvements for your city. Make a list of changes you think should be made.

"We think the city shouldn't allow cars in the downtown area on weekends. It would be nice to be able to walk around without worrying about traffic."

B Group work Compare your recommendations in groups. Choose the four most interesting recommendations and share them with the class.

Useful expressions

Making recommendations
The city should provide . . .
The city ought to . . . because . . .
Wouldn't it be nice if . . . ?
It would make a lot of sense to . . .

3 LISTENING & SPEAKING
Who's sorry now?

A Listen to a radio show called *Who's Sorry Now?* What is the focus of the show? Choose the correct answer.

- ☐ a. people's roommates in college
- ☐ b. things that people should or should not have done in the past
- ☐ c. family vacations

B Listen again. Are these statements true or false? Choose the correct answer.

	True	False
1. Mark made the manager think that Luke didn't want the job.	☐	☐
2. Mark said he should feel terrible, but he doesn't.	☐	☐
3. Anna buried her brother's harmonica in the desert.	☐	☐
4. Anna said she should have bought her brother a drum set.	☐	☐
5. Luke didn't tell his roommate that he knew about the call.	☐	☐
6. Luke thinks he should have told his roommate he knew about the call.	☐	☐

C Pair work Have you ever made a mistake like the ones on the radio show? Would you consider calling a show like *Who's Sorry Now?* to talk about it?

"Have you ever made a mistake like the ones on the radio show?"

"Well, when I was in college, I used to make up excuses so that I could avoid going to French class. I should have gone. I really wish I could speak French now."

"Would you call up a show like Who's Sorry Now?"

"I don't know. Maybe it would be fun. What about you?"

4 DISCUSSION
Welcome to my city!

A What are three places in your city that people would enjoy visiting? Make a list.

B Group work Tell your group facts about your city and its "must-see" places. Explain why they are worth seeing.

"Guadalajara, which is the second largest city in Mexico, has a lot of great markets. The Libertad Market is fantastic. It's a market every tourist should see because . . ."

4 EARLY BIRDS AND NIGHT OWLS

LESSON A ▶ It's about time!

1 STARTING POINT
What's your best time of day?

A Read these statements. How would you define the boldfaced words?

Teresa, South Africa
As soon as I get up in the morning, I race off to the gym. After I finish my workout, I head to the office. I always get there before any of my colleagues arrive. I suppose I'm a **morning person**.

Caio, Brazil
Ever since I was a kid, I've had trouble getting up early, so I guess I'm a **late riser**. Until I've had my coffee, I'm such a grouch. I'm not very approachable right after I wake up!

Mieko, Japan
I'm a **power napper**. While I take my lunch break at work, I often sneak a five-minute nap at my desk. After I have a little sleep, I feel great the rest of the day.

Richard, U.S.
I don't get much done until it gets to be late afternoon. Then I usually get a spurt of energy. I can concentrate best after everyone else has gone to bed. I'd say I'm a real **night owl**.

B Group work Which of the people in part A are you most similar to? Why?

2 DISCUSSION
The time is right.

A Pair work Read this information. Do you agree with the advice given? Why or why not?

When the Mind and Body Are at Their Best

Get on social networking sites between **8:00 and 9:00 A.M.**, when people tend to post more positive messages.

Energy levels drop between **1:00 and 4:00 P.M.**, and sleepiness is at its peak around **2:00 P.M.** This is a good time for a short nap.

Whenever you need to study for a test, do it in the **late morning**, when most adults perform their best.

Exercise between **4:00 and 7:00 P.M.**, when physical strength is at its greatest and risk of injury is at its lowest.

Whenever you have to work with numbers, plan to do it around **noon**, when thinking power is at its peak.

People can be most creative when they are less focused. Therefore, morning people are most creative in the evening, and night owls are most creative in the morning.

B Pair work Do you prefer to do these things in the morning, the afternoon, the evening, or at night? Why? Compare answers.

1. exercise   2. listen to music   3. study   4. speak English

3 GRAMMAR
Reduced time clauses

Notice how these clauses show time relationships. If the subject is the same in both clauses of the sentence, time clauses with *(right) before*, *(right) after*, and *while* can be reduced.

After I finish / **After** finishing my workout, I head to the office.
While I take / **While** taking my lunch break at work, I often sneak a five-minute nap.
I'm not very approachable **right after** I wake up / **right after** waking up!

However, other time clauses cannot usually be reduced.
Ever since I was a kid, I've had trouble getting up early.
As soon as I get up in the morning, I race off to the gym.
Until I've had my coffee, I'm such a grouch.
Whenever you have to work with numbers, plan to do it around noon.
I've been a night person **from the moment** I started college.

GRAMMAR PLUS see page 112

A Look at the Starting Point on page 28 again. Can you find more time clauses? Which one can be reduced?

B Pair work Complete the sentences with information about yourself. Then discuss your answers with a partner.

1. While working on a really difficult task, . . .
2. I don't feel awake in the morning until . . .
3. Whenever I have trouble sleeping, . . .
4. I can never concentrate after . . .
5. From the moment I wake up in the morning, . . .
6. As soon as I start to feel sleepy in the evening, . . .
7. Ever since I was young, . . .

"While working on a really difficult task, I have to stretch every 30 minutes."

4 VOCABULARY & SPEAKING
Energy and sleep

A Match the phrasal verb in the question with the correct definition.

1. Do you ever **burn out** from too much work? ____
2. How do you **calm down** after an argument? ____
3. How do you **chill out** after a rough day? ____
4. Do you ever **doze off** for a few minutes in public? ____
5. How do you **perk up** when you feel sleepy? ____
6. Do you **race off** as soon as class is over? ____
7. How often do you **sleep over** at a friend's? ____
8. What time do you **turn in** on the weekend? ____

a. become calm
b. get more energy
c. go to bed
d. lose all your energy
e. fall asleep for a short time
f. take it easy
g. stay for the night
h. go quickly

B Pair work Discuss the questions in part A. Ask follow-up questions.

"Whenever I feel like I'm going to burn out, I go for a bike ride to relax."
"That sounds like a good idea. Where do you like to ride?"

VOCABULARY PLUS see page 133

LESSON A   It's about time!

5 LISTENING & SPEAKING
Chilling out

A Stress can cause fatigue and a lack of energy. Select the things you do to cope with stress. Can you add other suggestions to the list?

- ☐ call a friend
- ☐ do yoga
- ☐ exercise vigorously
- ☐ get a massage
- ☐ listen to music
- ☐ take a hot bath
- ☐ vent your feelings
- ☐ _____
- ☐ _____

🔊 **B** Listen to Sean (*S*), Lisa (*L*), and Victor (*V*) talk about stress. What is the main cause of stress for each person? Write the correct letter.

____ too little time   ____ too much traffic   ____ too many responsibilities

🔊 **C** Listen again. What solution has each person found? Complete the chart.

	Solution
1. Sean	
2. Lisa	
3. Victor	

6 ROLE PLAY
I need some advice.

A Look at the problems below. Have you ever had problems like these? What other problems do people have with sleep and energy levels?

CALLER 1
I've been working day and night on an important project. It's going well, but I'm feeling so worn out. I'm worried about my health.

CALLER 2
I get so nervous before I have to give a presentation that I can't sleep the night before, and then I'm not at my best.

CALLER 3
I always put off studying until the night before a test. I stay up all night studying, but after that, I still don't do very well.

CALLER 4
Whenever my friends call or text me late at night, we chat for hours and hours. The next day, I can't keep my eyes open!

B Pair work Imagine you have one of the problems in part A. Take turns asking for and giving advice.

"I have a real problem. I've been working a lot on this project, and I'm so worn out. I'm worried about my health."
"So, how late do you usually work during the week?"
"I usually stay until 9:00 P.M. or so."
"Have you ever thought of telling someone that you need a little help?"

Useful expressions

Giving advice
Have you ever thought of (going) . . . ?
You might want to . . .
It might not be a bad idea to . . .
The way I see it, you ought to . . .

UNIT 4 Early birds and night owls

7 WRITING
Effective topic sentences

> Effective topic sentences are neither too general nor too specific. A topic sentence is supported by the other sentences in the paragraph.

A Read the paragraph. Then choose the best topic sentence from the list.

_____ Morning people jump out of bed in the morning, cheerful and full of energy. They seem to get most of their work done before lunch. On the other hand, night people have trouble getting up in the morning. They often drag themselves through the day and reach their peak in the evening. Night people, who often stay up until 2:00 or 3:00 A.M., are just getting started when morning people are going to bed.

a. Early morning is a bad time of day for most people.
b. Morning people and night people live very different lives.
c. Working at night is hard for morning people.
d. Night people get enough sleep even though they go to bed late.

B Read the paragraph and complete the topic sentence. Then compare answers with a partner.

Playing sports _____.
Usually, I play soccer or basketball. Kicking a soccer ball around clears my head. When I'm playing, I don't think about anything but the ball. Later, I feel relaxed, I'm focused, and I'm ready to concentrate on my homework.

C Choose one of these topics or your own idea. Then write a paragraph with a topic sentence.
- the best way to stay healthy
- an effective study plan
- earning extra money

D Pair work Take turns reading your paragraphs out loud, but don't read the topic sentence. Can you guess what your partner's topic sentence is?

LESSON B ▶ *Tossing and turning*

1 STARTING POINT
A good night's sleep

A Read the statements about sleep habits. Choose the statements that are true for you.

- ☐ I sometimes lie awake at night, even if I'm really tired.
- ☐ I'm lucky I can get by on six hours of sleep, considering that most people need eight.
- ☐ I'm a light sleeper, so any little noise wakes me up unless I'm really tired.
- ☐ I can manage on five hours of sleep, as long as I take a nap during the day.
- ☐ Unless I get a good night's sleep, I can easily fall asleep at school, at work, or even on the bus.
- ☐ I always set two alarm clocks just in case one of them doesn't go off.
- ☐ I only wake up early if I have somewhere to be in the morning.
- ☐ I never have any trouble sleeping.
- ☐ I'm exhausted every morning, even if I slept great all night.

B Pair work Compare your answers. Which statements are true for you?

"I definitely lie awake at night, even if I'm really tired. I can't help it. I replay everything that happened during the day."

"You're not the only one. I do the same thing, especially when I'm feeling stressed."

2 VOCABULARY
Expressions related to sleep

A Put these expressions about sleep in the correct columns. Then compare answers.

| be fast asleep | be wide awake | feel drowsy | nod off | take a power nap |
| be sound asleep | drift off | have a sleepless night | sleep like a log | toss and turn |

Having trouble sleeping	Falling asleep	Sleeping a short time	Sleeping deeply
			be fast asleep

B Pair work Use the expressions in part A to discuss your sleep habits and suggestions about sleeping better.

"Do you ever take a power nap during the day?"

"Not really. Whenever I try to take a nap, I end up sleeping until the next morning. But let me ask you something. What do you do when you feel drowsy after lunch?"

VOCABULARY PLUS see page 133

3 GRAMMAR

Clauses stating reasons and conditions

Even if introduces a condition that does not influence the main clause.
I sometimes lie awake at night, **even if** I'm really tired.

Considering that introduces causes and reasons that explain the main clause.
I'm lucky I can get by on six hours of sleep, **considering that** most people need eight.

As long as introduces a condition on which the main clause depends.
I can manage on five hours of sleep, **as long as** I take a nap during the day.

Unless introduces something that must happen in order to avoid a consequence.
Unless I get a good night's sleep, I can easily fall asleep at school, at work, or even on the bus.

(Just) in case introduces an undesirable circumstance that needs to be taken into account.
I always set two alarm clocks **(just) in case** one of them doesn't go off.

Only if or *only . . . if* introduces a condition that must be met for the main clause to be true.
I **only** wake up early **if** I have somewhere to be in the morning.
I wake up early **only if** I have somewhere to be in the morning.

GRAMMAR PLUS see page 113

A Look at the Starting Point on page 32 again. Can you find more clauses stating reasons and conditions?

B Match the clauses to make sentences. Then compare answers with a partner.

1. Drivers can fall asleep on the highway ____
2. Power naps at work are a good idea, ____
3. Some people set two morning alarms ____
4. I was surprisingly alert at work, ____
5. Night owls hate to wake up early, ____
6. I drink hot milk before bed only ____

a. if I've been having trouble sleeping.
b. even if it's a beautiful morning.
c. unless they rest before long trips.
d. as long as you have your boss's OK.
e. considering that I didn't sleep at all last night.
f. in case they sleep through one.

C Complete the sentences with information about yourself. Then compare answers with a partner.

1. Unless I have enough sleep at night, . . .
   I can't think very clearly in the morning.
2. I usually wake up on time, as long as . . .
3. I fall asleep pretty quickly at night, considering that . . .
4. I always have a boring book on my night table just in case . . .
5. Even if I'm extremely stressed out, I never . . .
6. I only leave a light on if . . .

LESSON **B** Tossing and turning

4 LISTENING & SPEAKING
I had the wildest dream.

A Listen to Kate and Sérgio talk about their recurring dreams. Whose dream do you think is scarier?

B Listen again. What is each person's dream? What do they think the dreams mean? Complete the chart.

	Dream	Meaning
Kate		
Sérgio		

C Pair work What do you think their dreams mean? Do you ever have similar dreams?

5 DISCUSSION
The meaning of dreams

A Read the information. Match the dreams with their possible meanings.

DREAMS
1. **Falling** You are falling through space, but you don't hit the ground or hurt yourself.
2. **Flying** You are flying and enjoying the sensation.
3. **Being chased** You feel as if someone is chasing you and you're in danger.
4. **Being embraced** Someone you like approaches you and hugs you.
5. **Losing teeth** Your teeth all fall out suddenly.
6. **Winning** You are successful in doing something.
7. **Being ashamed** You do something embarrassing and feel ashamed.

MEANINGS
a. You like someone and feel you can trust that person.
b. You feel very optimistic and proud about how your life is going.
c. You feel pleased with yourself and superior to other people.
d. You feel disappointed in yourself because of something you did.
e. You are worried about something, and this is a warning to be careful.
f. You feel out of control because someone is threatening you.
g. You feel insecure, and you are worried about losing something.

B Pair work Read these accounts of unusual dreams. What do you think they mean?

"Suddenly I found myself on stage in a school play and realized that I didn't know my lines. . . ."

"I was in a hot-air balloon above a big park. When I looked down, I was amazed to see hundreds of people on the ground pointing up at me. . . ."

"I was in a strange country and didn't know how I'd gotten there. I asked a man for help, and he held up a sign in a language I'd never seen before. . . ."

Useful expressions

Interpreting meaning
I think that means . . .
It sounds like . . .
The (balloon) probably stands for . . .
It might symbolize . . .

C Group work Finish each of the dreams. Take turns adding sentences.

6 READING
To sleep or not to sleep?

A Group work How many hours do you think people should sleep? Why? Discuss with your group. Then read the article.

To Sleep or Not to Sleep?

In the days before electricity, people didn't worry much about sleep. They usually went to bed a couple of hours after sunset and woke at sunrise. Even if they stayed up, there wasn't much to do in those days after the sun went down. But then came the electric lightbulb. And now we have the Internet, smartphones, stores that are open 24/7, and longer hours at work. How much can we sleep? How much should we sleep?

Like it or not, many of us are sleeping less on average. In 1910, most Americans slept nine hours a night. That dropped to seven hours by 2001. In 2009, a study by the National Sleep Foundation found that the average American got only 6.7 hours of sleep. The news is even worse for people who work the night shift. They sleep an average of just five hours.

Are we sleeping enough? Not if you believe in the old formula of eight hours of rest, eight hours of work, and eight hours of play. On the other hand, Neil Stanley, a British scientist who studies sleep, believes people's sleep needs vary. Some people need as many as 11 hours, but others need as few as three. How much do you really need? "To find out," he says, "simply sleep until you wake naturally, without the aid of an alarm clock. Feel rested? That's your sleep need."

Meanwhile, other scientists and pharmaceutical researchers are searching for new ways to keep us awake longer and prevent us from nodding off. A group of scientists is studying a gene found in some fruit flies that lets them get by on one-third the usual amount of sleep. Other researchers are developing chemicals that are more powerful than caffeine, the chemical found in coffee and tea. One experimental drug, CX717, kept laboratory monkeys working happily and accurately for 36 hours. Future breakthroughs may allow people to stay wide awake for several days straight.

The implications of this research are huge. On the one hand, this could lead to a world where we work longer and longer hours with less and less sleep. On the other hand, if we needed less sleep, we would have more free time for travel, sports, personal goals, and family.

To sleep or not to sleep — that may soon be the question.

B Read the article again. Then answer the questions.

1. What scientific research is mentioned in the article? What surprised you the most? What surprised you the least?
2. How much sleep does Neil Stanley think a person needs? Why?
3. What effects did the experimental drug mentioned in the article have on laboratory animals?

C Group work Discuss these questions. Then share your answers with the class.

1. Do you think you get enough sleep? What things keep you from getting more?
2. What do you think would happen if scientists found ways to let people stay awake longer? Would people be happier? Explain your answers.

5 COMMUNICATION
LESSON A ▶ *Making conversation*

1 STARTING POINT
Types of people you might meet

A Read about six different types of people you sometimes meet on social occasions. Match the descriptions with the pictures.

1. It's a good idea to try out different topics to get a conversation going, and the **conversation starter** does just that.

2. Talking about your accomplishments too much is often considered rude, but that doesn't stop the **braggart**.

3. Saying nice things about others is customary for the **complimenter**.

4. It's rude to ignore your conversation partner, but the **wandering mind** does it anyway.

5. Talking about topics that interest you is fun. Unfortunately, the **bore** is interesting to no one else.

6. It's usually considered impolite to interrupt people, but the **interrupter** is always jumping into the conversation out of turn.

a. Excuse me, let me say . . .
b. Hi. Are you enjoying the party?
c. I really enjoyed . . .
d. I'm absolutely the best tennis player.
e. That's a great tie!
f. So then I blah, blah, blah . . .

B Pair work Do you know any people like the six types above? What is it like to have a conversation with them?

"My best friend is kind of an interrupter. She's really nice, but I guess she just gets excited about the conversation and wants to jump in. It can be very annoying."

2 GRAMMAR

Infinitive and gerund phrases

It + be + adjective/noun + infinitive phrase is often used to comment on behavior.
These sentences can also be restated with gerund phrases.

It's rude to ignore your conversation partner.
It's a good idea to try out different topics.

Ignoring your conversation partner **is rude**.
Trying out different topics **is a good idea**.

The word *considered* may also follow *be* in this kind of sentence.

It's considered impolite to interrupt people.

Interrupting people **is considered impolite**.

These sentences can also include the phrase *for* + person/pronoun.

It's customary for the complimenter to say nice things about others.

Saying nice things about others **is customary for the complimenter**.

GRAMMAR PLUS see page 114

A Look at the Starting Point on page 36 again. Can you find more sentences that begin with gerunds? Try to change them into sentences beginning with *it's*.

B Rewrite the sentences using infinitive or gerund phrases. Then compare answers with a partner.

1. It's inappropriate to talk about politics at work or school.
   Talking about politics at work or school is inappropriate.
2. Using certain gestures is impolite in some foreign countries.
3. Asking someone's age is often considered rude.
4. It's not unusual in the U.S. to address a professor by his or her first name.
5. Hugging friends when you greet them is customary in many cultures.
6. Asking strangers if they're married is inappropriate in some countries.

3 VOCABULARY & SPEAKING

What's appropriate?

A Are these words and phrases positive (+), negative (–), or neutral (~)? Write the correct symbol next to each word.

___ 1. a compliment
___ 2. an insult
___ 3. appropriate
___ 4. bad form
___ 5. inappropriate
___ 6. normal
___ 7. offensive
___ 8. polite
___ 9. rude
___ 10. strange
___ 11. typical
___ 12. unusual

B Group work How do you feel about these things? Discuss these situations using the words and phrases in part A.

1. You kiss people on the cheek when you meet them.
2. You and your classmates interrupt the teacher.
3. You stand very close to people when you talk to them.
4. You and your parents talk honestly and openly.
5. Your best friend calls you after 11:00 P.M.
6. You start a conversation with a stranger on a bus or subway.

"It's unusual for me to kiss people I meet on the cheek."

VOCABULARY PLUS see page 134

4 ROLE PLAY
Making small talk

A Small talk is light conversation, often between people who don't know each other. Select the topics that are appropriate for small talk in your culture.

What's Safe for Small Talk?

- ☐ Children and family
- ☐ Current affairs
- ☐ Entertainment
- ☐ Health problems
- ☐ Hobbies
- ☐ Marital status
- ☐ Salaries
- ☐ Sports
- ☐ The weather

B **Group work** Imagine you are at a party. Start a conversation with one person, keep it going for one minute, and bring it to a close. Then find a new partner and repeat.

"Hi. How's it going?"
"Pretty good. Hey, did you see that soccer game last night?"
"I did! It's amazing to see our team play so well."
"I know! Hey, I should get going, but I'll call you later."

Useful expressions

Conversation openers	Conversation closers
How's it going?	See you later.
Can you believe this weather? It's (awful)!	Sorry, I've got to run. Talk to you soon.
That's a great (jacket).	It was great to meet you.
Do you know many people here?	I should get going. I'll call you later.

5 LISTENING
Party talk

A Listen to three conversations at different parties. Who is speaking in each one?

1. a. a mother and her son
   b. a teacher and her student
   c. a woman and her son's friend
2. a. two young students
   b. two older friends
   c. a father and his son
3. a. two cooks
   b. two wives
   c. two classmates

B Listen again. What closing phrase is used to end each conversation?

1. _____ 2. _____ 3. _____

6 WRITING
Organizing ideas with an outline

> Making an outline is a good way to organize your ideas before you write. An outline is usually written in reduced sentences or in notes and provides a general plan to follow when you write.

A Read the paragraph about a cultural rule in Japan. Then complete the outline below with information from the paragraph. What additional information is included in the paragraph but not in the outline?

Speaking on a cell phone in some public places in Japan is considered impolite. When receiving or making a cell phone call, most Japanese step away from the people around them. If that's impossible, it's customary to speak softly and use your hand to cover your mouth. Announcements on Japanese trains constantly remind passengers to switch their phones to silent mode. This is because people dislike being bothered by noise. Not everyone follows the rules, but most people do. The other day, people were glaring at me for taking a call in a café, and one person even scolded me. I was pretty shocked, but then I thought about it. Listening to others talking on the phone is irritating. There is a good reason why Japanese people use polite behavior when speaking on cell phones.

A. Topic sentence

Speaking on a cell phone in some public places in Japan *is impolite*.

B. Supporting sentences
- Recommended behavior:
  _____ or speak softly and cover mouth
- General example:
  Train announcements remind passengers – put phone on silent
- Personal example:
  People glaring for taking a call in _____

C. Concluding sentence

There is a good reason why Japanese people _____.

B **Pair work** Write an outline about a cultural rule from your country. Then exchange outlines and answer the questions.

1. Is the outline in a logical order?
2. Does the outline provide enough information? Is there anything else you would include?

C **Pair work** Use your outline to write a paragraph about the cultural rule. Then exchange paragraphs and answer the questions.

1. Does the paragraph follow the outline?
2. Is the cultural rule clear? What suggestions do you have to make it clearer?

LESSON A Making conversation

LESSON B ▶ It's personal.

1 STARTING POINT
Eavesdroppers

A Read each person's statement. What do you think they should do about each situation?

I Wish I Hadn't Heard That!

Luis, 23, Mexico City
"On the bus to work, I heard my boss's voice behind me. I think he was talking to the office manager on his cell phone. He was telling her that it would be a bad day at work. He explained that they were going to lay off my entire department!"

Rebecca, 25, Vancouver
"I overheard my roommate and her friend gossiping about me when I got home. I asked them what they were saying, but they claimed they hadn't been talking about me. I knew that wasn't true. It really hurt my feelings."

Pam, 18, Portland
"Last week, I overheard my little brother on his cell phone. He was warning his friend not to say anything. So of course I listened. He said he was getting a terrible grade in math this year! And he said it was a big secret, too. In fact, my parents still don't know the truth."

B **Group work** Have you ever heard someone talking about you? What did you do?

2 DISCUSSION
Who can you confide in?

A Read the information in the chart. Would you rank each person in the same way?

Who do you tell first?
We asked a group of young adults to rate each person in the chart according to when they would tell that person different types of personal news (1 = tell first, 4 = tell last). This is what they said.

Who would you tell . . .	Family member	Spouse	Close friend	Colleague
good news?	2	1	3	4
bad/tragic news?	1	2	3	4
gossip?	4	3	2	1
personal information?	3	2	1	4

Source: Interviews with people between the ages of 22 and 35

B **Pair work** Why would you tell something to one person and not to another? Discuss your reasons.

"I would usually talk about a personal problem with my close friends rather than my colleagues because my friends already know most of my secrets."

3 GRAMMAR
Reported speech

Statements	Reported statements
"It**'s** a big secret."	He said (that) it **was** a big secret.
"I**'m getting** a terrible grade."	He said (that) he **was getting** a terrible grade.
"They **got** engaged."	He said (that) they **had gotten** engaged.
"We **weren't talking** about you."	They claimed (that) they **hadn't been talking** about me.
"She**'s been** absent since Tuesday."	He said (that) she **had been** absent since Tuesday.
"We **had never been** there before."	She said (that) they **had never been** there before.
"I**'ll meet** you at the café."	He said (that) he **would meet** me at the café.

Questions	Reported questions
"**Did** you **know** about the layoffs?"	I asked him if he **had known** about the layoffs.
"What **are** you **saying**?"	I asked them what they **were saying**.

Commands	Reported commands
"**Don't say** anything!"	He warned his friend **not to say** anything.

General truths	Reported general truths
"The sun **rises** in the east."	She said (that) the sun **rises** in the east. (*No change in tense.*)

GRAMMAR PLUS see page 115

A Look at the Starting Point on page 40 again. Can you find more examples of reported speech?

B Rewrite the sentences using reported speech. Then compare answers with a partner.

1. "I'm not surprised at all."   She told me _____.
2. "Have you heard the news?"   He asked me _____.
3. "There's a bank down the street."   She said _____.
4. "Why aren't you talking?"   She asked me _____.
5. "Give him a call!"   He told me _____.
6. "We're getting married!"   She told me _____.
7. "Was the movie scary?"   The children asked me _____.
8. "We didn't take the 8:00 train."   They told me _____.

C **Pair work** Imagine that you have overheard this conversation. Take turns reporting each line of the conversation.

Ryan: I heard some interesting news. Do you know Amanda Jenkins?
Lara: I know what she looks like, but I've never met her.
Ryan: Well, she's going to study for a year in Australia.
Lara: How can she afford that?
Ryan: She got a scholarship that will take care of all her expenses.
Lara: I think that's great. When is she leaving?
Ryan: I don't know . . .

"Ryan told Lara that he'd heard some interesting news. He . . ."

LESSON B It's personal.

4 VOCABULARY & SPEAKING
Tell me what he said.

A Put these expressions for reported speech in the correct columns.

He claimed that . . .	He promised to . . .	He told me that . . .	He advised me to . . .
He asked me to . . .	He wanted to know . . .	He told me to . . .	He encouraged me to . . .
He warned me not to . . .	He explained that . . .	He asked me . . .	He wondered . . .

Statements	Commands or advice	Questions
He claimed that . . .		

B **Pair work** Tell a partner about a conversation you recently had. What was said? Use one of these topics or your own idea.

- an argument you had with a friend
- a time you asked someone for a big favor
- some exciting news a friend told you
- an apology you made or received

"My roommate claimed I had borrowed her sweater without asking, but I explained that . . ."

VOCABULARY PLUS see page 134

5 LISTENING
Tell me all about it!

A Listen to Nicole's and Tony's news. Choose the correct pictures.

1. Nicole

a. ☐   b. ☐

2. Tony

a. ☐   b. ☐

B Listen again. Choose the best answers.

1. Nicole's sister met her boyfriend . . .
   - ☐ a. in the fall.
   - ☐ b. yesterday.
   - ☐ c. over four years ago.

2. Nicole's sister is probably . . .
   - ☐ a. not afraid to be different.
   - ☐ b. very traditional.
   - ☐ c. shy.

3. How are things at the design studio?
   - ☐ a. There isn't enough work.
   - ☐ b. Things are picking up.
   - ☐ c. Everything's about the same.

4. Tony has been working at the studio . . .
   - ☐ a. longer than most other workers.
   - ☐ b. less time than most other workers.
   - ☐ c. as long as most other workers.

UNIT 5 Communication

6 READING
Mobile mania

A Read the article. These headings are missing from the text. Put them in the correct place.

- The Generic Ring
- The Distracted Driver
- The Useless Call Maker
- The I-Talk-Anywhere
- The Shouter
- The Corporate Big Shot

CELL PHONE PERSONALITY TYPES

In her travels, "Telephone Doctor" Nancy Friedman has noticed a variety of "cell phone personalities." Which of these types have you seen around?

1. The Shouter
Talking three times louder than necessary is characteristic of this offensive cell phone user. He seems to think everyone has a hearing impairment. Doesn't he know the phone already amplifies his voice?

2.
This pompous fellow makes all his business calls in public places while standing in the middle of a crowded room. He conducts big business deals right there in front of us, but we're not impressed.

3.
This exasperating person makes trivial phone calls, one after another, after another. On airplanes, you'll overhear her saying ridiculous things like, "Hi, we haven't left yet," or "Hi, we just landed. OK, see you in a minute."

4.
Making and taking calls anytime, anywhere is the trademark of this infuriating person. She'll chat in restaurants, at movie theaters, and even at funerals. When her cell phone rings, she looks at you and says insincerely, "Oh, sorry about that."

5.
Drive or use the phone – don't do both at the same time. This can be dangerous. It's really scary to see a delivery truck in the rearview mirror with a distracted driver on a phone behind the wheel.

6.
These are the people who haven't bothered to personalize their ring tone. One phone rings and 10 people check to see if it's theirs. Hang on, I think that's my phone!

Source: "What Type of Cell Phone User Are You?" by Nancy Friedman, www.telephonedoctor.com

B **Group work** Does the article describe any cell phone users you know or have seen? What bad cell phone manners have you seen recently?

LESSON B   It's personal.   43

6 WHAT'S THE REAL STORY?

LESSON A ▶ That's some story!

1 STARTING POINT
Weird news

A Read the news articles. Match each headline with the correct article.

a
CELL PHONE OPENS CAR DOOR

b
SEA LION
Paints for Her Supper

c
SURFING DOG
Upstages Rivals

1 The police have been called to a surfing contest in Brazil because a dog has been stealing all the attention. The dog became the main attraction at Praia da Tiririca in Bahia during the Surf World Championship. The dog and his owner surfed together on the same surfboard between the competitions. Police said, "They've called us to remove the pair because they've been getting more attention than the actual contest." The dog's owner said, "I've always surfed with my dog. He's always loved it. Sometimes I think he's a better surfer than I am!"

2 Maggie, a California sea lion at the Pittsburgh Zoo, has been amazing visitors by painting for her supper. She has created dozens of paintings. Her trainer said, "I started teaching her to paint last year, and she caught on quickly." Maggie spent three months learning to hold the paintbrush in her mouth and to touch it to the canvas. Adding the paint was the next step. Maggie earned a fish for every successful brushstroke. The trainer has saved all the paintings. She'll probably sell them to raise money to help animals.

3 A shopper in Michigan saved time and money after her husband helped her unlock her car from 10 miles away. After a day at the mall, the woman went out to her car, but couldn't find her keys. When she saw them still in the ignition, she called home and said, "I've locked my keys in the car. I've never done that before. I don't know what to do." Following her husband's instructions, she held her cell phone about a foot from the car door, while her husband held the spare car remote near his phone and pressed the unlock button. The door unlocked. She said, "I've totally stopped worrying about my keys now."

B Pair work One of the news stories isn't true. Which one do you think it is? (For the answer, see page 142.)

"I think story number one has got to be false. I just don't believe that a dog could surf. Story number two is also pretty amazing, but I have a feeling it's true."

44 UNIT 6 What's the real story?

2 GRAMMAR

Present perfect vs. simple past

Use the present perfect to report a recent event without giving a specific time reference.
I've locked my keys in the car.

Use the simple past to report an event with a specific time reference.
After a day at the mall, the woman **went out** to her car.
I **started** teaching her to paint **last year**.

GRAMMAR PLUS see page 116

A Look at the first story on page 44 again. Can you find more examples of the present perfect and the simple past? Why is each tense used?

B Complete the news story with the present perfect or simple past form of the verbs in parentheses. Then compare answers with a partner.

A group of thieves (1) **has stolen** (steal) the Dragon's Eye ruby from the Grand Gallery. Last night at about 1:00 A.M., the alarm (2) _____ (go off). Police (3) _____ (rush) to the building immediately, but they (4) _____ (be) too late. Right after learning of the robbery, the mayor (5) _____ (set up) a telephone hotline for information about the theft. Three people (6) _____ (call) so far, but the police are still looking for further information. They believe it is probable that the thieves (7) _____ (leave) the city. The curator of the Grand Gallery (8) _____ (offer) a $50,000 reward for information leading to the capture of the thieves.

3 GRAMMAR

Present perfect vs. present perfect continuous

Use the present perfect continuous to describe temporary situations and actions that are not yet completed. The present perfect describes permanent situations and recently completed actions.
A dog **has been stealing** all the attention. *(temporary situation)*
I've always **surfed** with my dog. *(permanent situation)*
Maggie **has been amazing** visitors by painting for her supper. *(not yet completed action)*
I've **locked** my keys in the car. *(recently completed action)*

Use the present perfect with the passive or with stative verbs such as *be*, *love*, and *have*.
He's always **loved** it.

GRAMMAR PLUS see page 116

A Look at the first story on page 44 again. Can you find another example of the present perfect continuous? Why is this form used?

B Complete the sentences with the present perfect or present perfect continuous form of the verbs in parentheses. Then compare answers with a partner.

1. Many residents **have been** (be) homeless ever since last month's storm and _____ (stay) with relatives while their homes are being repaired.
2. Although crews _____ (repair) the subway signals all week, they still _____ (not solve) the problem of long delays.
3. Police _____ (guard) the stores that the thieves _____ (not rob) yet.
4. Some organizations _____ (provide) free meals to residents, and will continue to do so all week.

LESSON A That's some story!

4 VOCABULARY & SPEAKING
It's in the news.

A How would you define each of these news events?

| epidemic | hijacking | natural disaster | rebellion | robbery |
| famine | kidnapping | political crisis | recession | scandal |

"A natural disaster is something like a volcanic eruption, a flood, or an earthquake."

B Pair work Tell your partner about some news stories you've recently heard. Use the words in part A.

"I saw something about a big scandal on the news this morning."
"Really? What was it?"
"Well, it said that a politician had been arrested for taking bribes."

VOCABULARY PLUS see page 135

5 LISTENING
Broadcast news

A Listen to an early morning news broadcast. What is each story about? Write the correct number.

___ a natural disaster   ___ a scandal   ___ an unusual family event   ___ an epidemic

B Listen again. Are the statements true or false? Choose the correct answer. Then correct the false statements to make them true.

	True	False
1. More people are suffering from TB than ever before.	☐	☐
2. Standard TB drugs are ineffective in about one-fourth of cases.	☐	☐
3. The painting *Sunflowers* was purchased by a large company.	☐	☐
4. The high price paid for the painting caused a scandal.	☐	☐
5. The hurricane has trapped some people in their homes.	☐	☐
6. Tourism in the area hit by the hurricane will not be affected.	☐	☐
7. The mother left the house to give her children freedom.	☐	☐
8. The children used food to get their mom down from the tree.	☐	☐

6 SPEAKING
Speaking of the news

A Pair work Discuss the questions. Ask follow-up questions and add extra information.

1. How closely do you follow the news? What kinds of stories interest you?
2. What do you think was the most important news story in the last few years?
3. Do you think stories about sports or celebrities count as "real news"?

B Group work Compare your answers with another pair. How are your opinions about the news different?

7 WRITING
Narratives

> A narrative is usually organized in chronological order and uses a variety of verb tenses.

A Number the events in this news story in the correct order. Then write a title for the article.

Title: _____

_____ As he was punching the shark, it began to release its grip on his leg.

_____ When the stunned shark finally let go, Anderson swam to shore, dragging his badly wounded leg behind him.

_____ He was pulling himself up on the rocks when another surfer came to his aid and called an ambulance.

_____ Anderson's leg was bleeding badly when emergency workers arrived, so they took him to a local hospital, where he was kept overnight for observation.

_____ In an interview shortly after Brian came home, his wife, also a surfer, said she knew her husband would surf again. However, she didn't know if she wanted her son to ever go back in the water!

_____ Doctors released Anderson the next day, and he spent the afternoon at home with his wife and son.

__1__ Brian Anderson was surfing at a popular spot south of Seaside, Oregon, on December 24, when he felt something was grabbing his leg.

__2__ Realizing it was a shark, he punched it repeatedly in the nose so it would loosen its grip.

_____ Anderson said he did this automatically because he'd heard on a TV show that sharks' noses are sensitive.

B Write a brief news story about a recent event. Use the simple past, present perfect, and present perfect continuous to show the order of events.

C Group work Take turns reading your stories. Ask follow-up questions. Who has the most interesting story? Why?

LESSON A That's some story!

LESSON B ▶ Storytelling

1 STARTING POINT
What happened?

A Pair work Read the stories. What do you think happened? Choose two stories and complete them by filling in the gaps indicated by ~~▶.

1 I went to the wrong class. It was the first day, so ~~▶. Afterwards, a classmate told me it was French IV and not my class, French I.

2 I'd picked up my mother's ring at the jeweler, but I couldn't find it when I got home. Up until then, I had never lost anything important, so I ~~▶. So, the ring wasn't lost after all! What a relief!

3 On my way home, I tried to take a shortcut through a neighbor's yard. As soon as I went through the gate, a huge dog suddenly ran up to me and ~~▶. Afterwards, we all laughed about it.

4 I had left for work a little earlier than usual. I got to the subway station, and ~~▶. When I got to work, my boss asked to speak to me. I knew he would never believe why I was late.

5 I volunteered to take care of my nephew. Before that, I'd never taken care of a toddler. As soon as his parents left, ~~▶. When they finally got home, the apartment, my nephew, and I were a mess!

6 Until some good friends invited me to a sushi restaurant, I had never had sushi in my life. When I put the first piece in my mouth, ~~▶. They were really nice about it, though.

B Group work Take turns sharing your stories. Have you had similar experiences?

2 LISTENING
How did it all end?

🔊 **A** Listen to two stories from the Starting Point. Which stories are they?

🔊 **B** Listen again. Choose the correct ending of each story.

1. ☐ a. He found the ring in his pocket.
   ☐ b. The jeweler had the ring.
   ☐ c. His mother found the ring.

2. ☐ a. The conductor helped her.
   ☐ b. A passenger helped her.
   ☐ c. The door finally opened.

48 UNIT 6 What's the real story?

3 GRAMMAR

Adverbs with the simple past and past perfect

Use these adverbs with the simple past to describe something that happened at a later time.
Afterwards, / **Later,** / **The next day**, we all **laughed** about it.

Use these adverbs with the simple past to describe two things that happened at the same time.
When / **As soon as** / **The moment** I **got** to work, my boss **asked** to speak to me.

Use these adverbs with the past perfect to describe something that was true or that happened before another event in the past.
Up until then, / **Before that,** / **Until that time**, I **had** never **lost** anything important.

GRAMMAR PLUS see page 117

A Look at the Starting Point on page 48 again. Can you find the adverbs from the grammar box? Which verb tenses are used after them?

B Write two sentences for these situations using the adverbs from the grammar box. Then compare answers with a partner.

1. My apartment was robbed last week.
   Up until then, I had never had anything stolen. The moment it happened, I called the police.
2. I moved into my own apartment this summer.
3. I failed my driving test last week.
4. I really enjoyed my trip to Singapore last month.
5. I was nervous about going to the dentist.
6. I knew I shouldn't have lent my friend my new laptop.

C Match the sentences with the illustrations. Then compare answers with a partner.

_b_ 1. This morning, I was on my way to work.
___ 2. Last night, I was telling a joke at a dinner party.
___ 3. I was backing my car out of the garage. I crashed into my neighbor's car.
___ 4. I got to the punch line. I knocked over a glass of water with my hand.
___ 5. She had never parked in front of my driveway.
___ 6. I noticed everyone laughing. I wasn't sure if they were laughing at the joke or at me.

D Pair work Take turns telling the stories for each picture. Use adverbs to show the order of events.

"This morning, I was on my way to work. I was backing my car out of the garage when I crashed into my neighbor's car. I couldn't believe it! Until then, she had . . ."

4 LISTENING
Embarrassing moments

A Listen to an interview with actor Dan Carville. What jobs does he talk about?

1. _____ 2. _____ 3. _____

B Listen again. Answer the questions.

1. Why did Dan lose his job at the department store?
2. Why didn't Dan last long as a painter?
3. Why was Dan fired from his job as a taxi driver?
4. How seriously do you think Dan took these jobs?

5 VOCABULARY & SPEAKING
Creating a story

A These phrases are used to tell a story. Put them in the correct columns.

I'll never forget the time . . .	Meanwhile . . .	To make a long story short . . .
The thing you have to know is . . .	And in the end . . .	I've got to tell you about . . .
It all started when . . .	That reminds me of when . . .	The other thing is . . .
What happened was . . .	The next thing we knew . . .	So finally . . .
I forgot to mention that . . .	So later on . . .	

Beginning a story	Continuing a story	Going back in a story	Ending a story
I'll never forget the time . . .			

B **Pair work** Tell a story about yourself. Use these story ideas and the phrases in part A. Ask follow-up questions.

STORY IDEAS
▶ You tried something for the first time.
▶ You did something really exciting.
▶ You forgot something important.
▶ You had a surprising experience.
▶ You met an unusual person.

"I'll never forget the first time I cooked a big dinner by myself. I had always helped my mother cook, so I thought it would be easy."
"Why were you cooking a big dinner?"
"Well, I had invited all my friends over, and . . ."

C **Group work** Share your story with another pair of students. Then choose one of the stories and tell it to the class.

VOCABULARY PLUS see page 135

UNIT 6 What's the real story?

6 READING
Personal anecdotes

A Pair work Look at the titles of the anecdotes. What do you think each one is about? Read the anecdotes to check your answers.

IT HAPPENED TO ME!
(or my friend . . . or a friend of a friend . . .)

Babysitter's Blues

I'll never forget the time last winter when I was babysitting these two kids for the first time. It was about 7:30 at night. Their mom had asked me to make them a pizza for dinner. It had been in the oven for about 15 minutes when suddenly I heard a noise outside, and the dog started barking. As soon as I opened the door and stepped outside, the kids slammed and locked it behind me. It was winter, and I stood outside freezing while they rolled around on the floor laughing hysterically. Meanwhile, the kitchen started getting smoky, and the smoke detector started buzzing. They didn't know what to do, so they let me back in. The pizza was burnt to a crisp. I didn't say anything. But, as we sat around the kitchen table having a bowl of cold cereal instead of their favorite, pizza, I could tell they regretted what they'd done. Anyway, to make a long story short, I babysit them all the time now, and guess what. I haven't had any problems since that first night.

– Amy Fernandez, Boston

A Bad Holiday

Have I learned any lessons the hard way? I sure have! What happened was I wanted a Monday off from work. Tuesday was a national holiday, and I thought a four-day weekend would be just perfect. I asked my boss, and he said no. At that company, all employees got their birthday off, so I asked if we could pretend that the Monday was my birthday. He said no. I woke up on the Monday morning feeling a little defiant, so I called in sick. I told them I got a terrible sunburn on the weekend. Later on, I realized that I had no color at all because I hadn't been out in the sun. So my friends and I went to the beach and stayed there all day. When I woke up the next morning, I had the worst sunburn of my life. I even had to go to the hospital! In the end, I learned a valuable lesson – I can't get away with anything!

– Rita Wagner, San Diego

B Group work Discuss these questions. Then share your answers with the class.

1. Why do you think Amy hasn't had any more problems?
2. What would you have done if you were Rita?
3. Which anecdote did you find more amusing? Why?

C Group work Choose one of the topics below, or one of your own, and tell your group an anecdote. Who had the most interesting anecdote? Whose was the funniest?

- celebrity encounters
- food experiences
- school days
- strange coincidences
- childhood memories
- mistaken identity
- speaking English
- travel stories

LESSON B Storytelling 51

COMMUNICATION REVIEW
UNITS 4–6

✓ SELF-ASSESSMENT

How well can you do these things? Choose the best answer.

I can . . .	Very well	OK	A little
▶ Describe how I deal with everyday problems (Ex. 1)	☐	☐	☐
▶ Describe a conversation I've heard or participated in (Ex. 2)	☐	☐	☐
▶ Understand the main points of an academic presentation about stress (Ex. 3)	☐	☐	☐
▶ Evaluate suggestions in a discussion about ways to deal with stress (Ex. 3)	☐	☐	☐
▶ Tell an interesting anecdote from my life (Ex. 4)	☐	☐	☐

Now do the corresponding exercises. Was your assessment correct?

1 SPEAKING
Calm down, chill out.

A What do you do in these situations?

1. Tomorrow is a big day – you have a job interview or an exam. You are worried that you won't sleep well.
2. You've been lying in bed for hours and can't get to sleep. You can't stop thinking about what you have to do tomorrow.
3. You feel angry about something a friend did.
4. You have been studying or working, and you need to take a break.

B **Pair work** Compare your answers with a partner. Are any of your solutions the same?

"Whenever I have something important the following day, I make sure I get some exercise so that I'll nod off as soon as I lie down."

2 SPEAKING
Guess what I heard!

A Read these situations. Can you think of a personal example for each one?

1. You overheard someone say something really funny.
2. Someone told you a big secret.
3. You realized something important.

B **Pair work** Discuss your answers with a partner.

"I was on the subway, and I overheard this guy tell his friend that he'd gotten into the bathtub the night before and realized he was still wearing his socks! I just burst out laughing."

3 LISTENING & SPEAKING
Stressed out!

A Listen to Dr. Phillips talking about stress. What is the main topic of his presentation? Choose the correct answer.

- ☐ a. the stress of living on a tight budget
- ☐ b. college students and stress
- ☐ c. stress and nutrition

B Listen again. Choose the causes of stress that are mentioned.

- ☐ 1. not having enough money
- ☐ 2. jobs
- ☐ 3. noisy roommates
- ☐ 4. too much studying
- ☐ 5. not enough studying
- ☐ 6. missing family

C Pair work Look at the causes of stress you chose and these suggestions for ways to deal with stress. Which do you think is the best suggestion? Why?

Ways to Deal with Stress

- Find a physical activity you enjoy and make time for it.
- Organize your time.
- Make time to relax.
- Eat breakfast. Don't drink too much coffee.
- Have a sense of humor.

"When you feel like you've got too much work, I think it's really important to sit down and organize your time. If you do, you'll feel more in control."

4 SPEAKING
Tell me a story.

A Pair work Tell your partner about a time when one of these things happened to you. Ask and answer follow-up questions so that you will be able to retell your partner's story. Take notes.

- You met someone fascinating.
- You did something that took a lot of courage.
- Something made you laugh hysterically.

B Group work Join another pair and tell your partner's story.

"Maria once met a famous marathon runner at a café. It was pretty crowded, and she had just sat down at the last free table. The next thing she knew, the runner walked up to her and . . ."

7 THE INFORMATION AGE

LESSON A ▶ A weird, wired world

1 STARTING POINT
Internet trends

A Look at these Internet trends. Choose the ones that affect you.

Internet Trends

NOW...
- ☐ Music fans have been given access to nearly unlimited music libraries in "the cloud."
- ☐ Increasingly, information about Internet users is being collected for marketing purposes.
- ☐ Many traditional textbooks have been replaced by online versions.
- ☐ With the development of new online tools, more employees are being allowed to work remotely for part of their workweek.

IN THE FUTURE...
- ☐ Most store purchases will be made by using a mobile device linked to an online account. Cash or credit cards will rarely be used.
- ☐ More and more doctor's examinations are likely going to be done over the Internet.
- ☐ More candidates for employment will be identified, interviewed, and hired online.
- ☐ The Internet is going to be subjected to a greater number of hacker attacks due to the increasing amount of personal information stored online.

B **Pair work** What did people do before these trends appeared?

"People used to buy CDs, and they put them in CD players to listen to them."

2 VOCABULARY
Technology buzzwords

A Match the terms on the left with the definitions on the right.

1. download ____
2. app ____
3. post ____
4. blog ____
5. Wi-Fi ____
6. the cloud ____
7. podcast ____
8. spyware ____
9. text ____
10. virus ____

a. wireless connection to the Internet
b. a radio or TV show downloadable from the Internet
c. transfer files to your computer or smartphone
d. harmful software that attacks computers or phones
e. send a short typed message from a cell phone
f. put something on the Internet for others to see
g. software that secretly records your online activity
h. a program often used on mobile devices
i. large, remote information storage areas on the Internet
j. an online journal or newsletter, usually of personal opinions

B **Pair work** Which of these technologies do you have experience with? When do you use them? Why?

"I've been downloading music and videos for years. And if I'm too busy to watch TV, I download podcasts of interesting shows to my smartphone. It's great!"

VOCABULARY PLUS see page 136

3 GRAMMAR

Passive of present continuous, present perfect, future

Use the passive for actions where the emphasis is on the object of the action.

Use the passive of the present continuous for ongoing actions.
More employees **are being allowed** to work remotely for part of their workweek.

Use the passive of the present perfect for recently completed actions.
Music fans **have been given** access to nearly unlimited music libraries in "the cloud."

Use *will* + passive or *be going to* + passive for actions that will begin in the future.
Most store purchases **will be made** by using a mobile device linked to an online account.
More and more doctor's examinations **are** likely **going to be done** over the Internet.

GRAMMAR PLUS *see page 118*

A Look at the Starting Point on page 54 again. Can you find more examples of each passive?

B Complete the sentences with the correct passive form of the verb in parentheses. Sometimes more than one answer is possible.

1. Thousands of computers already ___have been infected___ (infect) by spyware.
2. Currently, the cloud _____ (utilize) by a large number of businesses.
3. Thousands of blogs _____ (start) on all sorts of topics every day.
4. In coming years, even more fun game apps _____ (develop) for the youth market.
5. Nowadays, teen Internet use _____ (monitor) by concerned parents.
6. These days, podcasts _____ (download) by people of all ages.
7. Many computer viruses _____ (create) by teenagers.
8. In the future, Wi-Fi _____ (make) available in most public places.

4 LISTENING

Social networking: Different opinions

A Listen to three people's opinions about social networking. What do they mainly use it for?

1. _____   2. _____   3. _____

B Listen again. Choose the correct answers to complete the sentences.

1. Michael believes that social networking at work . . .
   - ☐ a. should be restricted.
   - ☐ b. makes workers happier.

2. In the case of children, Lisa believes that social networking . . .
   - ☐ a. teaches social skills.
   - ☐ b. is potentially harmful.

3. Daniel is careful about what he uploads or posts so people won't . . .
   - ☐ a. steal his work.
   - ☐ b. form a bad opinion of him.

LESSON A A weird, wired world

5 VOCABULARY
Connecting ideas formally

A These expressions connect ideas in different ways. Put them in the correct columns. Sometimes more than one answer is possible.

| additionally | as a result | for instance | in fact | nevertheless | similarly |
| as a matter of fact | for example | furthermore | likewise | on the other hand | therefore |

Add information	Compare or contrast	Emphasize	Give an example	Show a result
additionally				

B Choose the appropriate connector to complete the sentences.

1. Tom loves technology; *similarly / for example*, he has the latest cell phone.
2. Many airports offer inexpensive Wi-Fi; *nevertheless / in fact*, at some it's even free.
3. Many of my friends' computers have been damaged by viruses; *nevertheless / therefore*, I am going to update my antivirus software.
4. Some websites aren't reliable; *as a result / likewise*, many people are being misinformed.
5. Few people could have predicted recent advances in Internet technology; *for example / likewise*, predicting the future of the Internet is difficult.
6. Internet identity theft is something very serious; *on the other hand / as a matter of fact*, it can ruin your life.

VOCABULARY PLUS see page 136

6 DISCUSSION
Social networking debate

A **Pair work** Do you think social networking sites are a positive or negative influence? Find a partner who has the same opinion.

B **Group work** Find a pair who disagrees with you and your partner. Take turns explaining your reasons. Each pair gets a chance to disagree.

"The way I see it, social networking sites are a positive influence because they allow me to have friends all over the world."

"That may be true, but in my opinion, online friends aren't really true friends. In fact, . . ."

Useful expressions		
Expressing opinions	**Disagreeing**	**Giving reasons**
If you ask me, . . .	That may be true, but . . .	That's why . . .
The way I see it, . . .	I see your point, but . . .	The reason for that is . . .

UNIT 7 The information age

7 WRITING
Writing a product or service review

> Writing and posting a product or service review helps other consumers make informed decisions. Most product and service reviews contain similar features.

A Look at the information about product reviews. Then read the review below and select the things the review does. Find examples in the review with a partner.

- ☐ 1. names the product and explains its use
- ☐ 2. explains where it can be purchased
- ☐ 3. mentions positive features
- ☐ 4. suggests how it could be improved
- ☐ 5. states who would find it useful and why
- ☐ 6. gives the exact price

Organize Me XPS is one of the best tools I have used for managing my busy schedule – and I have used many over the years. With this app, I'm able to organize all of my tasks and appointments in one place with just a couple of simple steps. Furthermore, a simple set-up is all it takes to share my plans with others. Having the ability to share my lists and calendars with colleagues and friends like this is extremely useful.

The only drawback some people might find is that it does not have all of the features offered by some of the more expensive productivity apps; nevertheless, it does exactly what I need it to do. In fact, the app's simplicity is its best feature. I just love the simple interface. Although the developers promise that free updates offering new features will be released soon, if you ask me, the low cost makes it a really good value as is.

If you're someone who writes notes on little pieces of paper and then loses them, get this app. It will really boost your productivity. I use it every day – for school, work, and everything else.

B Use one of these topics or your own idea to write a product or service review.

- technology you purchased
- a game or app you tried
- a restaurant you ate at
- a service you used (dry cleaner, hair salon, mechanic)

C Group work Take turns reading your reviews. Then answer the questions.

1. Whose review is the most interesting and informative? Why?
2. What additional information would you want to know as a consumer?
3. Which reviews would convince you to buy the product or use the service? Which ones would lead you to make a different choice?

LESSON A   A weird, wired world

LESSON B ▶ Information overload

1 STARTING POINT
Future shock

A Read these comments about technology. Do you agree or disagree?

WHAT'S Your TAKE ON TECHNOLOGY?

Joo-chan, Seoul:
"Apps are cool, aren't they? I download lots of them to my smartphone. Wouldn't it be great if phones came loaded with even more apps?"

Ana, São Paulo:
"Isn't it weird how some people use mobile devices constantly? They don't notice anything around them. It's actually dangerous, don't you think?"

Sarah, Los Angeles:
"Don't you think there are too many websites full of misinformation? Shouldn't the government fine sites that contain false information?"

Yang Ming, Taipei:
"Doesn't it seem like kids spend too much time playing violent video games? It makes kids more aggressive, doesn't it?"

B Pair work Compare your answers with a partner. Do you think the government should regulate any of these things?

2 VOCABULARY
Forms of communication

A Where do you find these forms of communication? Put them in the correct columns. Then add another expression to each category.

| banner ads | bumper stickers | crawls | infomercials | spam | text messages |
| billboards | bus wraps | fliers | pop-up ads | telemarketing | voice mail |

On television	On the Internet	On the phone	On streets or highways

B Pair work Which of the above are the most useful ways of communicating information? The least useful? Do you find any of them annoying?

"Those crawls at the bottom of TV screens aren't useful. It's impossible to read them and pay attention to a show at the same time. Don't you think they're annoying?"

VOCABULARY PLUS see page 136

UNIT 7 The information age

3 GRAMMAR

Negative and tag questions for giving opinions

Use negative questions or tag questions to offer an opinion and invite someone to react.
Isn't it weird how some people use mobile devices constantly?
Doesn't it seem like kids spend too much time playing violent video games?
Wouldn't it be great if phones came loaded with even more apps?
Shouldn't the government fine sites that contain false information?
Apps are cool, **aren't they**?
It makes kids more aggressive, **doesn't it**?

Use the phrase *don't you think* to form negative or tag questions for opinions.
Don't you think there are too many websites full of misinformation?
It's actually dangerous, **don't you think**?

GRAMMAR PLUS see page 119

A Look at the Starting Point on page 58 again. Find the tag questions used by Joo-chan and Yang Ming. Why do they have different endings?

B Pair work Turn the statements into negative or tag questions. Then ask and answer the questions. Discuss your answers.

1. It's annoying how often telemarketers call.
2. They should get rid of those banner ads on the Internet.
3. It would be great if there were fewer billboards.
4. It seems like a lot of people are texting while driving.
5. It's sad when people are tricked into losing money by spam messages.
6. There are too many channels on TV these days.

4 DISCUSSION

It's kind of strange, isn't it?

A Pair work Do you agree or disagree with these opinions? Why?

- Millions of people are addicted to online games these days. It's kind of sad, isn't it?
- Wouldn't it be great if the Internet were turned off one day a week to give people a chance to rest?
- Don't you think a lot of people are being confused by misinformation on the Internet?
- Aren't kids today being exposed to too much information on television and on the Internet?
- Don't you find it annoying that social networking sites sell your personal information to marketers?

B Group work What other problems are caused by modern information technology? Agree on the three most pressing problems and tell the class.

"Don't you think kids today spend too much time online? Won't their grades and social development suffer because of it?"

"You might be right. But their parents should set limits for them, shouldn't they?"

LESSON B Information overload

5 LISTENING
Health and technology

A Listen to a report on health problems caused by technology. Who is the main intended audience? Choose the correct answer.

- ☐ a. doctors or other health professionals
- ☐ b. frequent users of technology products
- ☐ c. designers of computers and mobile devices

B Listen again and complete the chart.

Problem	Symptoms	Advice
texter's thumb		
carpal tunnel syndrome		
gadget addiction		

6 DISCUSSION
Future technologies?

A Read about these technologies. Are any of them available now? Do you think any will be available in the future? Would you like to make use of them? Why or why not?

Technologies of Tomorrow?

You'll never be bored with the color of your clothes or furniture again. With color-changing fabric, you'll be able to select from a wide variety of colors using a remote control, changing colors whenever you want.

Wireless electricity will allow you to do away with chargers, batteries, and cords. Devices and appliances in homes and businesses will run on electricity transmitted wirelessly from a hidden power source.

A life recorder is a small wearable device that will take a video of everything you see, twenty-four hours a day, seven days a week. The sights and sounds of your entire life will be saved for years to come.

B Group work What new technologies are becoming popular? Which ones do you think are useful? What other technologies do you think will be invented in the future?

7 READING
Cyber-begging

A **Pair work** Imagine that a stranger asked you for money to help pay off a frivolous debt. Would you help? Tell your partner. Then read the article.

Can you spare a dime for my Gucci bills?

There was a time when Karyn Bosnak couldn't pay a $59.00 bill at the grocery store. She was officially broke. She didn't have enough money to get on the subway, but she looked rich. She was a television producer, earned $900 a week, and had a closetful of designer labels like Gucci and Louis Vuitton. But she also had a $20,221.40 credit card bill and an empty bank account. Karyn decided that it was time for a change. She built a website and simply asked people to help her out by sending her a buck or two.

On the site, Karyn honestly explained her situation, Gucci shoes and all. "If 20,000 people gave me just $1, I'd be home free, and I'm sure there are 20,000 people out there who can afford to give me $1." Amazingly, it worked. Her website was visited by more than a million people. Although most donors just gave a few dollars, one generous donor sent $1,000. She was on TV and in newspapers and magazines. She was offered a book deal and a movie contract. And of course, she was able to pay off her credit card debt.

She also sold her designer clothes on eBay. In her closet, where the Gucci purses once sat, Karyn keeps all the letters that people have sent her.

She's received teddy bears, subscriptions to *Vogue*, Dunkin' Donuts coupons, backpacks, jewelry, cat food, and candles.

It's hard to understand why so many people helped a total stranger pay off her huge credit card bill. Why did they do it? Karyn explains, "I was just honest about what happened; I didn't make up some sob story about saving the world." Her donors think it's funny and original, she argues, and view it less as a charity than as an entertainment site.

Imitators have sprung up all over the Internet, some with outrageously selfish requests like a BMW or a house. Actually, Karyn was not the first person to put up a website asking strangers for money. The practice has a name: "cyber-begging." Most sites receive little traffic and even less cash.

Karyn also had thousands of enemies and critics. People sent her hate mail and scolded her on websites. Karyn says she never let this anger bother her. "They are probably jealous they didn't think of it," she explains.

Source: "Brother, can you spare a dime for my Gucci bills?" by Janelle Brown, Salon.com

B Read the article again and answer the questions. Then compare your answers with a partner.

1. Why was Karyn in financial trouble?
2. What was her main solution to her problem? What else did she do?
3. Why did so many people respond positively to her website?

C **Group work** Discuss these questions. Then share your answers with the class.

1. Do you think Karyn was unethical, or was she simply clever?
2. What would you have done if you were Karyn?

LESSON B Information overload

8 PUTTING THE MIND TO WORK

LESSON A ▶ Exploring creativity

1 STARTING POINT
Creative professions

A Pair work How much creativity do you think these jobs require? Number them from 1 (most creative) to 4 (least creative). Explain your choices.

____ chef   ____ surgeon   ____ photographer   ____ jazz musician

"I think a chef has to be the most creative. Inventing new dishes requires a lot of creativity."

B Group work Which jobs might be right for these kinds of people? Discuss your answers.

1. someone able to think quickly
2. a person looking for adventure
3. people good with their hands
4. someone needing job security
5. a person trained in music
6. a person with a good voice

"Someone able to think quickly might be a good surgeon. You never know what might go wrong once the operation starts."

2 VOCABULARY
Creative qualities

A What qualities do creative people usually have? Complete the chart with the correct nouns or adjectives.

Noun	Adjective	Noun	Adjective	Noun	Adjective
curiosity	*curious*	innovation			passionate
decisiveness		knowledge		patience	
	determined		motivated		perceptive
	disciplined		original		resourceful

B Pair work Which of the qualities in the chart are most important to your job or studies? Discuss with a partner.

"Well, I'm studying engineering, and we get a lot of assignments, so I have to be very disciplined. It's a very competitive field."

VOCABULARY PLUS see page 137

3 GRAMMAR

Reduced relative clauses

You can shorten a relative clause by dropping the relative pronoun and the verb *be*.
Someone (**who / that is**) **able to think quickly** might be a good surgeon.
A person (**who / that is**) **looking for adventure** could be a private detective.
A person (**who / that is**) **trained in music** might be a good DJ.

You can also drop *who / that* and change the verb to the gerund.
Someone **who / that needs job security** might not want to be a jazz musician.
Someone **needing job security** might not want to be a jazz musician.

In many relative clauses, *who / that* + the verb *have* can be replaced by *with*.
A person **who / that has a good voice** could be a good TV journalist.
A person **with a good voice** could be a good TV journalist.

GRAMMAR PLUS *see page 120*

A Look at the Starting Point on page 62 again. Can you make the reduced relative clauses in part B into full clauses? What verb forms do the full clauses use?

B Rewrite these sentences with reduced relative clauses. Then compare with a partner.

1. Someone who hopes to be a chef should get the proper training.
   Someone hoping to be a chef should get the proper training.
2. Anyone who wants to be an actor needs both talent and luck.
3. A person who works as a comedian is always looking for new ways to make people laugh.
4. People who are clever enough to get inside the mind of a criminal would make good detectives.
5. Anyone who dreams of becoming a champion athlete has to be prepared to do a lot of hard work.
6. Someone who is interested in the latest music trends might be a good DJ.
7. A person who is responsible for a large staff has to be able to be creative with scheduling.

C Complete these sentences using reduced relative clauses and your own ideas.

1. . . . needs to take voice lessons.
   Someone dreaming of becoming a professional singer needs to take voice lessons.
2. . . . should speak English as much as possible.
3. . . . should keep up with current events.
4. . . . doesn't need to have a good speaking voice.
5. . . . should follow the latest trends in clothing.
6. . . . has to study the behavior of animals.
7. . . . usually have a great love of food and eating.
8. . . . will find the job market extremely competitive.

LESSON A Exploring creativity

4 DISCUSSION
Creativity quiz

A How creative are you? Complete the quiz.

How Creative Are You?

	Always	Sometimes	Rarely	Never
1. Are you a risk taker?	3	2	1	0
2. Are you naturally curious?	3	2	1	0
3. Do you look for opportunities to improve things?	3	2	1	0
4. Are you sensitive to beauty?	3	2	1	0
5. Do you challenge accepted ideas?	3	2	1	0
6. Do you keep an eye out for new fashions and products?	3	2	1	0
7. Do you adapt easily to new situations?	3	2	1	0
8. Do you trust your guesses, intuitions, and insights?	3	2	1	0
9. Are you more interested in the future than in the past?	3	2	1	0
10. Do you have a creative sense of humor?	3	2	1	0

B **Pair work** Add up your score. Then check what your score means below. Do you agree? Why or why not? Tell your partner.

About You	21–30	11–20	0–10
	Because you're open-minded, you like to keep up with the latest trends and innovations. Accepting the status quo bores you. You see mistakes as learning experiences.	You often have good ideas, but you prefer to feel them out with friends before taking action. You're up-to-date with new fashions and products, but unlikely to be the first in your group to try them.	You prefer to stick with the tried-and-true, which helps you feel safe, but you may get left behind in later years. You're content with who you are and what you know.

5 LISTENING
Creativity at work

🔊 **A** Listen to Samira, Alex, and Naomi talking about their occupations. What does each person do?

🔊 **B** Listen again. What do Samira (*S*), Alex (*A*), and Naomi (*N*) say they focus on in their work? Write the correct letter.

____ 1. helping indecisive clients   ____ 4. solving a wide variety of problems
____ 2. efficiency   ____ 5. new ideas to replace rejected ones
____ 3. beating the competition   ____ 6. using old concepts in new ways

6 WRITING
Beginning new paragraphs

> Begin a new paragraph each time you change the focus of your ideas.

A Read this composition. The writer changes focus twice. Indicate with a *P* where the two new paragraphs should begin. Then compare answers with a partner.

Lucy Gomez is the most creative person I know. She started piano lessons when she was only four years old. At school, she was always creating interesting projects in her art class. When she was only 12 years old, she won a citywide poetry contest. Her parents were very proud of her. Lucy works as a sitcom writer for a popular TV show now. She works with a group of writers, and together they have to think of original ideas for stories. They also have to come up with funny dialogue for the actors on their show, because the actors have to play believable characters that will make the audience laugh. It is not an easy job, but Lucy does it well. She starts work late in the morning and often works until 7:00 or 8:00 at night. Lucy is very curious. She likes to travel and meet new people who have opinions that are different from hers. And she's always noting ideas, drawing quick sketches, and taking photos. She tells me that doing these things helps her turn new experiences into a source of ideas for her work. I always enjoy talking to her and am happy to know someone as knowledgeable and creative as Lucy.

B Brainstorm ideas for a composition about someone who is very creative or who is unique or different in an interesting way. Answer these questions to help you.

1. In what ways is this person special or different?
2. How does this affect his or her life?
3. Would you like to be like this person? Why or why not?

C Write a three-paragraph composition based on your ideas.

D **Pair work** Read your partner's composition and answer these questions.

1. Do the paragraphs start and end where they should?
2. Is the focus of each paragraph clear?
3. Is there any additional information you would like to know that was not included?

LESSON A Exploring creativity

LESSON B ▶ Ideas that work

1 STARTING POINT
Everyday objects

A Read about these unusual uses of everyday objects. Have you ever used them in these ways?

Three Clever Ideas

1 "I have three cats, which means there's usually a lot of cat fur on my clothes. To get rid of the fur, I wrap my hand in tape, sticky side out. Then I rub the tape over my clothes, and it picks up the fur!"

2 "The zipper was stuck on my favorite jacket. Luckily, my roommate works in fashion, which is great because she knew how to fix it. She just rubbed a drop of olive oil on the zipper."

3 "Tacos can be messy to eat, which is why I wrap them in paper coffee filters. I serve them that way at parties and backyard barbecues. It works great for other messy sandwiches, too!"

B Group work Use your imagination to suggest new uses for these everyday items. Decide on the best use for each and share it with the class.

- old newspapers
- a shower curtain
- aluminum foil
- empty shoe boxes
- dental floss
- a hair dryer
- empty jars or cans
- rubber bands

"You can wrap green tomatoes in newspaper to make them ripen more quickly."

2 VOCABULARY & SPEAKING
Exploring possibilities

A Combine the verbs with the nouns to make common expressions.

Verbs			Nouns			
analyze	find	organize	a decision	a problem	a solution	possibilities
explore	make	solve	a mistake	a situation	alternatives	information

analyze a situation, solve a problem, . . .

B Pair work Discuss the questions. Then ask your partner more questions using the new vocabulary.

1. When do you make decisions quickly? When do you explore the possibilities first?
2. Who do you talk to when you need to find a solution to a big problem? Why?
3. When was the last time you analyzed a mistake you made? What did you learn from it?

VOCABULARY PLUS *see page 137*

UNIT 8 Putting the mind to work

3 GRAMMAR

Non-defining relative clauses as sentence modifiers

You can use non-defining relative clauses with *which* to make a comment about an entire sentence.
I have three cats, **which means there's usually a lot of cat fur on my clothes**.
My roommate is a slob, **which is why I want to get my own apartment**.

GRAMMAR PLUS see page 121

A Look at the Starting Point on page 66 again. Can you find more examples of these grammar patterns? How are the commas used?

B Match these statements with the appropriate non-defining clauses. Then compare with a partner and write two similar statements of your own.

1. I want to give away all my old books, _h_
2. I had locked my keys in my car, ____
3. I've been exploring possibilities for natural cleaners, ____
4. My son made a robot costume for himself, ____
5. Our neighbor saves her empty jars for my dad, ____
6. I downloaded a great new app that helps me organize information, ____
7. It's easy to get lost when driving in a new city, ____
8. Adam has bought some expensive software to edit videos, ____

a. which is why you saw me opening it with a coat hanger.
b. which is great since he uses them to store nails and things in his workroom.
c. which is great because I think it's solved my problem of forgetting where I store files.
d. which is why I was wiping lemon juice and salt on those copper pots.
e. which is one reason why GPS systems were developed for cars.
f. which is why he was covered in aluminum foil yesterday.
g. which is strange since there are plenty of free programs that do that well.
h. which means I have to get boxes for them.

4 SPEAKING

Key inventions

A What inventions or discoveries do you think have had the greatest impact on modern life? Make a list.

the cell phone   *the television*   *the airplane*

B **Group work** Compare lists with your group.

"I think the cell phone has really affected people's lives. People can talk wherever they are, which means they can always be in touch and save time."

5 LISTENING
Great ideas

A Look at the pictures. What do you know about these products or services? How do you think they were developed?

B Listen to these stories about the invention and development of the products in the photos. Complete the chart.

	Bill Bowerman	Fred Smith
How he got the idea		
The initial reaction to the idea		
What the inventor did in response		

6 DISCUSSION
Making life better

A **Pair work** Why do people create or invent new products? Read this list of reasons and add two more of your own.

- to help protect people's health
- to make business more efficient
- to make daily life easier
- to make life more enjoyable
- to protect the environment
- to save lives
- _____
- _____

B **Group work** Join another pair. Why do you think these things were created or invented? Use the reasons in part A or others of your own.

1. air conditioners
2. artificial sweeteners
3. digital cameras
4. electric knives
5. hybrid cars
6. karaoke machines
7. laptops
8. lie detectors
9. scanners

"I think air conditioners were invented to protect people's health. The summer heat can be deadly for infants and the elderly."

UNIT 8 Putting the mind to work

7 READING
A unique inventor and his invention

A Read the title of the article. What do you think Daisuke Inoue invented? Then read the article and check your answer.

The Man Who Taught the World to Sing

Daisuke Inoue was a drummer in a band near Osaka, Japan, that played versions of famous pop songs. People loved to sing along as the band played, but most of them couldn't carry a tune. Inoue's band had spent years learning how to make the untalented customer sound in tune by adjusting the music to match the customer's voice. The singers, mainly Japanese businessmen out for a night on the town, loved Inoue's unique follow-along style.

In 1971, a loyal client asked Inoue to escort him on a company trip, but Inoue could not attend. He found a solution: he recorded his band's back-up tracks, and then hooked up a car stereo and an amplifier. With this device, Inoue gave birth to the karaoke machine. By the 1980s, *karaoke*, which means "empty orchestra," was a Japanese word that required no translation across the globe.

Unfortunately, Inoue never bothered to patent the world's first karaoke machine, so he lost his chance to become one of Japan's richest men. When asked if he regretted not patenting his invention, 65-year-old Daisuke Inoue confessed, "I'm not an inventor. I am just resourceful. I simply put things that already exist together. Who would consider patenting something like that?"

Inoue's friend Robert Scott Field says, "Some people say he lost 150 million dollars. If it were me, I'd be crying in the corner, but he's a happy guy. I think he's amazed to find that he's touched so many lives." Inoue believes the little box he put together has had a huge social impact, especially in Japan. At weddings and company get-togethers, the karaoke comes out and people relax. It breaks the ice.

Although Inoue spent years in obscurity, in 1999, *Time* magazine called him one of the twentieth century's most influential people, saying he had "helped to liberate the once unvoiced."

Inoue is always getting asked silly questions, but he takes them in stride. "Women approach me all the time and ask if I can help their husbands sing better. I always say that if her husband were any good at singing, he would be making a living at it. He's bad, which means he's just like the rest of us."

Inoue didn't use a modern karaoke machine until he was 59 years old, but his favorite English songs are "Love Is a Many Splendored Thing" and Ray Charles' "I Can't Stop Loving You." "They're easy, which is good because I'm a terrible singer," said Daisuke Inoue, the man who taught the world to sing.

Source: "Mr. Song and Dance Man," by Dr. David McNeill, Sophia University, Tokyo

B Group work Discuss these questions. Then share your answers with the class.

1. What led Daisuke Inoue to create his invention? Do you agree he was only being resourceful, or was he actually an inventor? Explain.

2. Would you have the same attitude as Inoue if you invented something popular and received no compensation? Why or why not?

3. How do you think Inoue "helped to liberate the once unvoiced" both as a drummer in his band and as the inventor of karaoke? Do you think this is a good thing? Explain.

9 GENERALLY SPEAKING
LESSON A ▶ How typical are you?

1 STARTING POINT
What's typical?

A Read about the "typical" person in Italy and Japan. What information surprised you? Why?

The typical ITALIAN person...	The typical JAPANESE person...
drinks **155 liters** of bottled water per year.	drinks **10 liters** of bottled water per year.
consumes **3.2 kilograms** of coffee per year.	consumes **1.4 kilograms** of coffee per year.
consumes **0.1 kilograms** of tea per year.	consumes **0.9 kilograms** of tea per year.
visits the doctor **6 times** per year.	visits the doctor **14 times** per year.
watches **27 hours** of TV per week.	watches **21 hours** of TV per week.
gets married at **30 years old** (for men) or **27 years old** (for women).	gets married at **30 years old** (for men) or **27 years old** (for women).
studies for **7.2 years** after the age of 15.	studies for **9.5 years** after the age of 15.
travels **710 kilometers** by rail per year.	travels **1,900 kilometers** by rail per year.

Source: www.nationmaster.com

B Complete these statements. Use information from the chart.

1. Unlike the Japanese, Italians seem to drink a lot of _bottled water_.
2. While the typical _____ person studies until the age of 22, the typical _____ person studies until the age of 24.
3. Both like TV, except that the typical _____ person watches more.
4. In contrast to Italians, the Japanese travel a lot more _____.
5. Both groups are fairly different, except for the age _____.

2 SPEAKING
That's just so typical!

A Pair work What are typical examples of these things in your hometown?

1. a store   2. a home   3. a job   4. a car   5. a snack food   6. a weekend activity

B Group work Join another pair and compare your answers.

"What's a typical store in your hometown?"
"We have something called 'dollar stores.' They have household goods, clothes, toys, and lots of other stuff. And everything's really inexpensive."

3 GRAMMAR

Clauses and phrases showing contrast and exception

Use *while*, *unlike*, and *in contrast to* in order to present contrasting information, especially in writing.
While the typical Italian person studies until the age of 22, the typical Japanese person studies until the age of 24.
Unlike the Japanese, Italians seem to drink a lot of bottled water.
In contrast to Italians, the Japanese travel a lot more by rail.

Use *except (that)*, *except (for)*, and *except for the fact (that)* to show an exception.
Both like TV, **except (that)** the typical Italian person watches more.
Italian and Japanese people are fairly different, **except for** the age they get married.
Japanese people typically consume less, **except for the fact that** they drink more tea.

GRAMMAR PLUS see page 122

A Look at the Starting Point on page 70 again. Notice the sentences in part B that use phrases with *except*. Which phrase is followed by a clause?

B Here's some information about customs. How are they different in other places? Write sentences showing contrasts and indicating exceptions.

1. When people in the U.S. go to a party, they usually arrive a few minutes late.
   Unlike people in the U.S., most people where I live arrive on time for parties.
2. Most people in Canada have cereal and milk for breakfast some days of the week.
3. Most people in the U.S. who study a foreign language in college choose Spanish.
4. In the U.K., it's common for friends to split the bill at a restaurant.
5. For people in Italy, lunch is the main meal of the day.
6. Women in Spain usually kiss people on both cheeks when they meet.

C Are you typical? Complete these sentences and compare with a partner.

1. Unlike most people where I live, *I don't own a car.*
2. In contrast to most of my friends, . . .
3. While a lot of the people where I live . . .
4. I'm similar to many of my friends, except that . . .

4 DISCUSSION

Are you typical?

Group work Choose the answer that makes each sentence true for you. Then compare answers with your group. Are you typical in your group?

Are you typical?

1. I need *six or less / seven / eight or more* hours of sleep.
2. For commuting, I rely mainly on *buses / subways / trains / taxis / a car*.
3. I tend to eat *healthy / unhealthy* snacks between meals.
4. I spend the most time with my friends *in person / on the phone / online*.
5. I button my clothes from the *top down / bottom up*.
6. A great night out should include a *movie / play / concert / sporting event*.

"Unlike most of the people in my group, I need eight or more hours of sleep or I don't feel rested. Most people in my group need only six hours or less."

5 VOCABULARY
Should I just go with the flow?

A Are these adjectives, verbs, and phrases related to accepting things as they are or to making changes? Put them in the correct columns.

Adjectives	Verbs	Phrases
amenable	accept	be your own person
conservative	conform (to)	fit in
rebellious	confront	follow the crowd
(un)conventional	stand up (to/for)	make waves

Accepting things as they are	Making changes

B Group work Use the expressions in the chart in part A to describe what you think these people might be like. Give examples to explain your ideas.

1. Ed, a guy who gets along with everyone
2. Clarissa, an actor desperate for attention
3. Rob, an assistant at a law firm hoping for a promotion
4. Diana, a leader who wants to change the world

"Ed is probably amenable and does what other people want. I imagine he only confronts people if he really has to and generally follows the crowd."

VOCABULARY PLUS see page 138

6 LISTENING & SPEAKING
How are they different?

A Listen to Yoshiko, Diego, and Suzanne talking about their school experiences. Answer the questions.

1. What examples does Yoshiko give for how she is typical? In what way is she different?
2. What are three ways that Diego's life is typical? In what way doesn't he follow the crowd?
3. Does Suzanne give an example of how her life is unconventional? If so, what is it?

B Listen again. Do Yoshiko, Diego, and Suzanne believe they are typical or different from most people their age?

C Pair work Do you tend to go with the flow or be your own person? Discuss these questions.

1. Are your interests similar to those of your friends and family or different? Explain.
2. In what ways do the clothes you wear make you stand out or fit in?
3. How does your taste in music compare to that of other people your age?

Yoshiko in Mexico

7 WRITING
Supporting statements

> Supporting statements develop the topic sentence by providing key facts, reasons, or examples.

A Read the paragraph. What's the topic sentence? Underline three supporting statements that develop the main idea in the topic sentence. Then compare your answers with a partner.

Unconventionally Cool: Trendspotter Josie Buchier

June 13

My friend Josie Buchier doesn't like to follow the crowd. While most of us are trying our best to fit in with everyone else, Josie likes to be her own person. For instance, she has her own unique sense of fashion, so she likes to buy all her clothes, except for her shoes, in used clothing shops. Her taste in music is also pretty unconventional. Unlike most of my friends, she can't stand pop music. She prefers to listen to Philippine and Andean folk music. She also has a very interesting job. Unlike her old nine-to-five job in a conservative department store, she now works as a trendspotter for an advertising company. This means that she spends her time looking at the latest fashion and entertainment trends among young people. Then she writes reports for her company about what's in style. This makes my unconventional friend a trendsetter that others follow, and that's pretty cool.

[4 comments]

B Finish these statements with information of your own to make topic sentences. Compare with a partner.

1. Generally speaking, most people where I live don't . . .
2. One of my best friends is . . .
3. In general, my friends tend to be . . .

C Choose one of the topic sentences and brainstorm supporting ideas. Then choose at least four supporting statements and write a paragraph.

Generally speaking, most people where I live don't mind making waves. It's their way of . . .

D **Pair work** Exchange paragraphs and answer these questions.

1. Do all the supporting statements relate to the topic sentence?
2. Do they develop and explain the topic sentence?
3. Do the supporting details fit together in a logical order?
4. What other facts, reasons, or examples could be added?

LESSON B ▶ Problems and solutions

1 STARTING POINT
I never used to feel stressed.

A Read Annie's email to her friend. What problems does she have?

To: Adriana Costa
From: Annie Wilson
Subject: Missing you!

Hi Adriana,

How are things back in Cartagena? Are you glad to be home again? Sorry I haven't written lately. I have a lot of new responsibilities at work now, so I've been really stressed. My job didn't use to be so demanding!

I have to say, I miss you. You used to be such a good influence on me! These days, I oversleep. I'm even late for work sometimes! That never used to happen because I knew I had to meet you at the café in the morning. I remember how you would complain about the coffee they served. You used to call it "brown water"!

I'm spending too much money, too. Every time I go to the mall, I see something I want to buy. That's another reason I miss you! I would see some great jacket, but you wouldn't let me buy it. You would always tell me I didn't need it and drag me away!

Also, I have a noisy new roommate, Cindy. All she ever does is gab on her cell! Remember the way we would sit around talking? You always used to make me laugh. I bet that's a big reason I never used to feel stressed like I do now!

Anyway, the weekend will be here soon, so I'm sure I'll feel better then.

Write soon!
Annie

B Pair work What do you think Annie should do about her problems?

"Annie should find another friend to meet at the café in the morning."

2 VOCABULARY
Expressions with *keep* and *stay*

A Match the phrases to make questions. Notice the expressions with *keep* and *stay*.

1. When you're stressed, can you **keep** _e_
2. When friends move away, do you **keep / stay** ___
3. If you're sleepy while studying, what can you do to **stay** ___
4. What news sources do you read in order to **keep** ___
5. Do you break the rules or do you **keep / stay** ___
6. How do you save money when you need to **keep** ___
7. Is it important for old friends to **keep / stay** ___

a. expenses down?
b. up with current events?
c. connected?
d. in touch?
e. things in perspective?
f. awake?
g. out of trouble?

B Pair work Take turns answering the questions. Discuss your answers.

VOCABULARY PLUS see page 138

UNIT 9 Generally speaking

3 GRAMMAR

Past habitual with *used to* and *would*

Used to and *would* can both be used to describe past habitual actions or situations which are no longer true. However, *would* cannot be used with stative verbs such as *live*, *be*, *have*, or *like*.

You always **used to make** me laugh.
My job **didn't use to be** so demanding!
Remember the way we **would sit** around talking?
I **would see** some great jacket, but you **wouldn't let** me buy it.

GRAMMAR PLUS see page 123

A Look at the Starting Point on page 74 again. Make a list of the things that have changed for Annie since Adriana went back to Colombia.

B Complete these sentences with *used to* or *would*. Sometimes more than one answer is possible.

The first year of high school, I wasn't a very good student. I (1) ___**used to**___ think school was boring. I remember my classmates (2) _____ go to the library and work on projects or study, but I (3) _____ like to play video games at a friend's house instead. We (4) _____ go right after class, and we (5) _____ spend three or four hours doing that. My parents both (6) _____ have jobs with long hours, so they never knew what time I (7) _____ get home. I thought I was smart, and that I didn't need to study to keep my grades up. But one day, I was asked to go to the principal's office. He said, "You (8) _____ be a great student. Now your grades are terrible. Explain!" That was a real wake-up call. After that, I became serious about school, and I (9) _____ study and finish my homework before playing video games. Now that my kids are in high school, I tell them about all the silly things I (10) _____ do when I was their age.

4 DISCUSSION

Personal concerns

A Pair work These people have had a change in their lives. What positive or negative impacts have these changes had?

Lucas Santos, 25, Curitiba
"Before my wife and I had our first baby, we would go out whenever we wanted. We can't do that now. I didn't use to be a worrier, but I am now."

Britney Majors, 32, Toronto
"Before my promotion, I would eat lunch in the cafeteria because that was all I could afford. Now I have money to go to nice cafés, but I just don't have the time. So, I usually eat at my desk."

Wen Ho Chen, 67, Taipei
"We used to plan on moving in with our son when we retired. But we've changed our minds. We just sold our house, and we're going to travel the world."

B Group work Think about a big change in your life. Talk about the positive and negative impacts it had.

"Last year, I was transferred to another department in my company. My new responsibilities are a lot more interesting, but I didn't use to have to work this much."

LESSON B Problems and solutions

5 LISTENING & SPEAKING
Different approaches to problem solving

A **Pair work** Read about these three approaches to problem solving. What method do you use? Give examples to support your answer.

What kind of problem solver are you?

Different people solve their problems in different ways. The three main approaches are assertive, meditative, and cooperative. Find out which one best describes you.

▶ **Assertive** people prefer action to talk. When they're faced with a problem, they immediately try to work out a solution.

▶ When **meditative** people have a problem, they sit and think about it, and might even do research. Sometimes, the answer comes to them if they don't act on something right away.

▶ **Cooperative** people think the easiest way to solve a problem is to ask for help. Another person's perspective can help cooperative people come up with solutions.

"I'd say I'm a meditative person. Before I bought my first car, I spent hours doing research on it by myself. It took me forever to decide!"

B Listen to Dominique, Carla, and Wayne talking about their personal concerns. What kind of problem solver is each person?

C Listen again. What are two things each person did to solve their problem?

6 ROLE PLAY
Here's an idea . . .

A Read about these people's problems. What advice would you give each person?

- My boss is so demanding. She gives me more work than I can handle.
- I can't save money because I always spend it on little things I want but don't really need.
- My last job interview went very badly. I always get tongue-tied in front of authority figures.
- I'm not enjoying things like I used to. I'm not sure why. Maybe I'm too stressed.

B Role-play each situation. Take turns giving and receiving advice.

"My boss is so demanding. She gives me more work than I can handle."

"Here's an idea. See if your co-workers feel the same way. Maybe you all can talk to the boss about it."

"I guess I could try that."

Useful expressions	
Giving advice	**Receiving advice**
Here's an idea . . .	I guess I could try that.
If I were you, I'd . . .	I just might try that.

UNIT 9 Generally speaking

7 READING
Creative problem solving

A Pair work Look at these paintings of the same landscape. How are they different? What effect does this have on what you notice first? Discuss. Then read the article.

Painting and Problem Solving: FOUR LESSONS

Earlier this month I escaped the office for a weeklong painting retreat in the woods of Door County, Wisconsin. While working amidst the awe-inspiring fall colors, it occurred to me that the dynamics of painting and problem solving have a lot in common. I returned home not only with newly polished painting skills but also a fresh perspective on managing problems. I learned four lessons while painting:

1 How you see things depends on your line of sight. When painting a landscape, countless choices are yours. For starters, you can choose where to place the horizon and what you eliminate from the actual setting. If the existing landscape is cluttered, for instance, you can exclude elements that detract from your focal point. Likewise, in problem solving, getting caught up in the clutter diminishes your ability to reach your desired result. Choose instead to focus on the bigger picture.

2 People can see the same landscape and represent it in totally different ways. One day I sat with two other painters in a microclimate with magnificent sugar maples. Much to my surprise, our final paintings were totally different. A similar phenomenon occurs in problem solving: Any number of people can arrive at the same situation with different ideas, skills, or resources. They can also have different designs on the end result. In this way, respecting where others are coming from is critical to problem solving.

3 When light is shined on a subject, you can explore what lies in the shadows. It can be harder to paint landscapes on cloudy days. The various forms and contrasts are less clear, and it's difficult to explore what lies in the shadows. When the sun is shining, however, the distinctions between objects are clearly visible and what lies in the shadows is revealed. The same goes for problem solving: When you shine a light on an issue, you see everything more clearly, including what opportunities or threats exist in the shadows.

4 Collaborating with people at different levels can foster appreciation for diverse ideas and perspectives. At the retreat, there were painters at every level, from first-timers to fine artists. I learned something from each one, particularly when our group came in from the woods and worked together in the studio. I opened myself up to others' unique observations and feedback, and ultimately felt more energized and creative. Additionally, I was struck by our instructor's capacity to calibrate her critiques to our individual skill levels. Similarly, in problem solving, it's important to meet others where they are, not where you might want them to be.

Odds are there is a problem on your desk today. How might even one of these four lessons help you brush up your problem-solving skills?

Source: "4 Ways to Brush Up Your Problem-Solving Skills," by Barbara T. Armstrong

B Group work Discuss these questions. Then share your answers with the class.

1. In what way is it helpful to avoid paying attention to details when solving a problem?
2. How are the second and fourth lessons in the article similar?
3. What do you think the author means by "shine a light on an issue"? How is this helpful?
4. How can the lessons from the article help you solve one of your own problems?

COMMUNICATION REVIEW
UNITS 7–9

SELF-ASSESSMENT

How well can you do these things? Choose the best answer.

I can . . .	Very well	OK	A little
▸ Describe how information technology has changed people's lives (Ex. 1)	☐	☐	☐
▸ Describe how new technologies will change people's lives (Ex. 2)	☐	☐	☐
▸ Understand the main points of a phone conversation about personality types (Ex. 3)	☐	☐	☐
▸ Describe my personality type (Ex. 3)	☐	☐	☐
▸ Describe and compare typical behavior of parents and teenagers (Ex. 4)	☐	☐	☐

Now do the corresponding exercises. Was your assessment correct?

1 DISCUSSION
How things have changed!

A Think about how information technology has changed in the past few years. How have people's shopping habits, hobbies, and social lives been affected?

B Pair work Compare your answers with a partner.

"Video games used to be low-tech and expensive. Some games used to be available on the Internet, but few people would play them. Now, a lot of people play video games online. I think they've been greatly improved, and many are fairly cheap."

"Yeah, I think so, too. But too much time is spent playing them. My whole family is addicted – even my grandmother plays! She used to think video games were a waste of time when I played them as a kid."

2 DISCUSSION
What next?

A Pair work What do you think will happen in the next 10 years as a result of new technologies in these areas?

1. communication
2. education
3. entertainment
4. finance
5. medicine
6. sports

B Group work Compare your predictions in groups.

"Ten years from now, I think cell phones will be used by everyone. They'll even be used at work instead of office phones. What do you think?"

3 LISTENING & SPEAKING
Team roles: The perfect "STEAM" team

A Listen to the phone conversation between Tony and Annie. What is Tony's agency doing? Choose the correct answer.

- ☐ a. They're exploring the possibilities of using cell phones in advertising.
- ☐ b. They're analyzing the effectiveness of their advertisements.
- ☐ c. They're working to improve a company's image.

B Listen again. Match the roles on the left with the personality types on the right.

Role	Personality type
1. Solver _d_	a. disciplined
2. Team manager ___	b. patient
3. Explorer ___	c. passionate
4. Analyst ___	d. creative
5. Motivator ___	e. resourceful

C Pair work Look at the roles again. Which role do you think you would be best at or would enjoy most? Why? Compare your ideas with a partner.

"I think I'd probably be best in an Explorer role. I'm pretty resourceful. What about you?"

"I'm a person with a lot of patience, but I'm not that creative. I'm more of a Team manager type."

4 SPEAKING
That's so typical!

A Complete this chart with your opinions about typical parents and teenagers.

	The typical parent	The typical teenager
What are some of their concerns?		
What is their most valued possession?		
How much time do they spend with friends?		
What do they use the Internet for?		
What do they like to do on vacation?		

B Write at least four sentences contrasting the typical parent with the typical teenager. Then compare with a partner.

"Generally, the typical teenager is concerned about friends, while the typical parent is concerned about his or her children."

10 THE ART OF COMPLAINING
LESSON A ▶ That really bugs me!

1 STARTING POINT
Everyday annoyances

A Have you ever had problems similar to these? Do you agree or disagree with these comments? Why?

"The thing that I hate is when kids ride their scooters on the sidewalk."

"One thing that bothers me is when my friends don't show up on time for things."

"Something that bugs me is people who take up two seats on a crowded bus."

"The thing I can't stand is co-workers who leave their cell phones ringing on their desks."

B Group work Look at the situations in part A. Would you complain, or would you be quietly annoyed? Why?

2 LISTENING & SPEAKING
It really irks me!

🔊 **A** Listen to Jane and Kyle talking about irritating situations. What bothered each person?

🔊 **B** Listen again. Discuss the questions.

1. Whose situation do you think was more annoying, Jane's or Kyle's?
2. Who do you think handled the situation better, Jane or Kyle?
3. How would you have reacted in each situation?

3 GRAMMAR

Relative clauses and noun clauses

A relative clause can occur in the subject or the object of a sentence.
Something **that bugs me** is people **who take up two seats on a crowded bus**.
The thing (**that**) **I can't stand** is co-workers **who / that leave their cell phones ringing on their desks**.

Some sentences use a relative clause and a noun clause beginning with a question word such as *when*.
The thing (**that**) **I hate** is **when kids ride their scooters on the sidewalk**.
One thing **that bothers me** is **when my friends don't show up on time for things**.

GRAMMAR PLUS see page 124

A Look at the Starting Point on page 80 again. Which clauses are relative clauses? Which are noun clauses?

B Pair work Complete the sentences with your own opinions. Then discuss them with a partner.

1. One thing that irks me about my neighbors is . . .
   when they park too close to my car.
2. Something that bothers me about my friends is . . .
3. If I'm riding in a car, something that irritates me is . . .
4. The thing that aggravates me most is a friend . . .
5. The thing that annoys me about people talking on cell phones is . . .
6. . . . is one thing that bothers me at home.

4 VOCABULARY

That drives me up the wall!

A Combine the verbs with the phrases. How many combinations can you make? How are their meanings different?

Verbs	Phrases			
drive	on someone's nerves	someone mad	someone upset
get	someone crazy	someone sick	someone's blood boil
make	someone down	someone up the wall	under someone's skin

B Group work How do these things make you feel? Discuss these situations using the expressions in part A.

1. people laughing at their own jokes
2. vending machines that "steal" your money
3. finding empty ice cube trays in the freezer
4. people eating on public transportation
5. airlines not serving food on long flights

"The thing that drives me crazy is when people laugh at their own jokes, and they're not funny!"

VOCABULARY PLUS see page 139

LESSON A That really bugs me!

5 DISCUSSION
Polite complaints

A Which of these descriptions fits you best? Give examples to support your answer.

> I very rarely complain.

a silent sufferer

> I only complain if I absolutely have to.

a calm, collected type

> I complain because it's my right.

an activist

> I complain about every little thing.

a whiner

"I guess I'm a silent sufferer. For example, I never complain in a restaurant, even if the food is awful."

"You don't? Bad food in a restaurant really annoys me. I always complain! I mean, why should I pay for terrible food? I guess I must be an activist."

B Pair work What would you do or say in these situations? Compare your answers.

1. A taxi driver is playing the radio loudly while you are trying to make a phone call.
2. Your neighbor's young son tore up all the flowers in your garden.
3. You see someone littering in a public park.

"If the taxi driver were playing the radio very loudly, I think I'd just speak louder. I probably wouldn't say anything to the driver. But I wouldn't give him a very good tip either."

6 ROLE PLAY
I hate to mention this, . . .

A Pair work Use the language in the box to create polite complaints for each situation. Then take turns acting out your complaints for the class.

1. You've been waiting in line for a long time, and someone suddenly cuts in front of you.
2. You've had a party, and one friend is still at your home long after everyone else has left. It's driving you up the wall because it's really late, and you need to get up early.
3. After you've been waiting patiently for your food for an hour, the waiter brings you the wrong order.
4. Every time you go out with your friend, she asks you to hold her belongings because she doesn't carry a bag. It's really beginning to get on your nerves.

> **Useful expressions**
>
> **Complaining to strangers**
> Excuse me, but . . .
> I'm sorry, but . . .
>
> **Complaining to friends/neighbors**
> I hate to mention this, but . . .
> I'm sorry to bring this up, but . . .

B Group work Which complaints were the most effective? Which were the most polite?

7 WRITING
Messages of complaint

Writing an effective message of complaint is a powerful way to solve an ongoing problem with a product or service.

A Match the information to the points in the email.

Writing an effective message of complaint
An effective message of complaint about a purchase...

1. contains a clear subject line.
2. describes the product or service clearly.
3. explains the problem in detail.
4. mentions a receipt or other evidence.
5. explains exactly what you want.
6. provides contact information.

To: customerservice@phonegrp.cup.org
From: JM1990@cup.org
Subject: Damaged product — 1

Dear Sir or Madam:

Last month, I ordered a smartphone, model number VG25S, from your website. When it arrived, I discovered that it was broken. The case was damaged, and the display screen was cracked.

At my own expense, I returned the phone to your service department over a month ago. I still have not received a replacement, nor has a customer service representative contacted me.

I have my credit card bill to prove I paid for this purchase, a one-year warranty, and a receipt from the post office. Therefore, I would like to receive a new phone as soon as possible.

Please call or email me about this matter. I look forward to your reply and hope you will handle this matter promptly.

Sincerely,

John Montgomery
101 Bee Tree Road
Encino, CA 91426
Phone: 310-555-2934

B Write an email complaining about one of these situations or one of your own.

- Your tablet came with the wrong battery charger, but you didn't notice until you brought it home. You called the store, and they refused to replace it.
- You bought airplane tickets in advance, but the airline had overbooked the flight, and you couldn't get on the plane.

C Pair work Take turns reading your emails. Did your partner follow all the steps for writing an effective message of complaint?

LESSON B ▶ Let's do something about it!

1 STARTING POINT
Why don't they do something about it?

A How many of these problems have you experienced? Compare with a partner.

"Overcrowded buses really make me mad. I wonder why they don't have more buses at rush hour."

"Umbrellas are so poorly made these days. I don't know why they always break in the wind."

"My cell phone never works around here. I can't understand why the reception is so bad."

For service in English, press 1.

"Automated phone menus drive me crazy. What I don't get is why companies don't have people answer their phones."

"The clothes in those shops are unbelievably expensive. How anyone can afford them is beyond me."

"The college course I want is really popular. My big concern is whether I'll be able to get into the class."

B **Pair work** Which of the problems in part A bother you the most? Explain.

"Broken umbrellas definitely bother me the most. That happened to me just the other day."

"You can say that again. I just hate it when that happens."

> **Useful expressions**
>
> **Agreeing and showing sympathy**
> I know (exactly) what you mean.
> Yeah, I hate that too.
> You can say that again.

2 LISTENING
If this is correct, say, "Yes."

A Have you ever had problems with automated phone menus? What happened?

🔊 **B** Listen to Gabriel using an automated phone menu. Is he successful? Choose the best summary.

☐ a. He completed his business successfully and will pick up his prescription this evening.

☐ b. He can't fill his prescription because the machine didn't recognize what he said.

☐ c. His pronunciation is so poor that the system didn't understand anything he said.

🔊 **C** Listen again. Answer the questions.

1. What's the name of the store?
2. What is his prescription number?
3. What is his phone number?
4. What time does he want to pick up his prescription?

3 GRAMMAR

Simple and complex indirect questions

Simple indirect questions use statement word order and begin with expressions such as *I wonder, I'd like to know*, or *I can't understand*.

Why don't they have more buses at rush hour?   I wonder why **they don't have** more buses at rush hour.

Complex indirect questions also use statement word order. In addition, they begin or end with clauses or phrases with *be*.

Will I be able to get into the class?   **My big concern is** whether I'll be able to get into the class.
How can anyone afford them?   How anyone can afford them **is beyond me**.

GRAMMAR PLUS see page 125

A Look at the Starting Point on page 84 again. Can you find more indirect questions? Which ones are simple indirect questions? Which are complex?

B Rewrite these questions using the words in parentheses. Then compare answers with a partner.

1. Will airlines ever stop losing passengers' luggage? (I wonder . . .)
   I wonder if airlines will ever stop losing passengers' luggage.
2. How do I correct a mistake on my phone bill? (I'd like to know . . .)
3. Why can't I use my cell phone in an elevator? (The thing I don't get is . . .)
4. How can I get tickets to sold-out concerts? (I want to find out . . .)
5. When will the government deal with global warming? (I'd like to know . . .)
6. Why do people complain so much? (. . . is something I can't understand.)

4 VOCABULARY & SPEAKING

I'm totally baffled!

A Look at these words that describe feelings. Put them in the correct columns.

| annoyed | confused | depressed | enraged | humiliated | insulted | mystified | stunned |
| baffled | demoralized | discouraged | frustrated | infuriated | irritated | saddened | |

Confused feelings	Angry feelings	Sad feelings
baffled	*annoyed*	

B Pair work Complete the sentences with your own information. Then discuss your answers with a partner.

1. I'm totally baffled by . . .
2. I get so infuriated when . . .
3. I always get discouraged when . . .
4. I wouldn't be demoralized even if . . .
5. I remember feeling stunned when . . .
6. I would feel insulted if . . .

"I'm totally baffled by people who can speak a lot of languages. How do they remember so many different words and grammar rules?"

VOCABULARY PLUS see page 139

LESSON B   Let's do something about it!

5 DISCUSSION
A word to the wise

A Pair work Read the advice about how to avoid consumer problems. Can you add any more ideas to the list?

Buyer Beware!
SMART ADVICE FOR SMART SHOPPERS

- Buy from a reputable company.
- Make sure there's a guarantee.
- Examine your purchases before you buy.
- Do some comparison shopping.
- Find out about the return policy.
- Find out how the item should be cared for.

B Group work Discuss a time when you had a problem with something you bought. Would the advice in part A have helped you?

"I bought some really expensive luggage last month, and I was enraged when, after just a week, one of the wheels came off."
"Oh, you're kidding. Did you take it back to the store?"
"Yes, but they told me I couldn't return it because I'd bought it on sale. I should have asked about their return policy . . ."

Useful expressions
Sympathizing
Oh, you're kidding.
That's ridiculous.
What a pain.

6 ROLE PLAY
I'd like to return this.

A Read the store returns policy in part B. Is there a similar policy at the stores where you shop?

B Pair work Take turns role-playing a customer and a clerk at a returns counter. Use the returns policy and the situations below.

STORE RETURNS POLICY: All items must be in good condition and accompanied by a receipt. No cash refunds; store credit only. No items returned after two weeks unless under warranty. No return of items purchased on sale or with coupons.

Situation 1
- T-shirt
- have receipt
- shrank after washing
- now too small

Situation 2
- laptop
- receipt at home
- defective
- still under warranty

Situation 3
- camera
- lost receipt
- not very user-friendly
- want to exchange

"I'd like to return this T-shirt, please. I can't understand why it shrank after I washed it."
"I wonder whether you followed the washing instructions properly."
"I certainly did!"
"That's fine, then. May I see your receipt, please?"

7 READING

The power of one voice

A Pair work What steps would you take if someone damaged one of your valuable possessions? Discuss with a partner. Then read the article and find out what Dave Caroll did. Did he take any of the steps you discussed?

Dave Carroll Airs a Complaint

Dave Carroll was ready to quit his 20-year career as an independent musician. Then, an airline broke his guitar and changed his life.

The airline wouldn't budge on Dave's request for $1,200 in flight vouchers to cover repairs to his $3,500 Taylor guitar. When he got "The Final No!" email after nine months of negotiations, he wrote back to say he wasn't without options.

Dave said that if he were a lawyer, he might have sued the airline, but as a songwriter, he had other tools at his disposal. He vowed to write two or three songs, make a music video for each one, and post them on YouTube.

"After months of feeling frustrated and angry about the ordeal, for the first time I felt empowered, as though a weight had been lifted from me. I changed gears from someone who *wanted* something to someone who was going to *do* something."

His goal was to reach one million views in the next year. Four days after he posted the first video, he hit a million views. The airline called him a day after the video was released to offer the same $1,200 in flight vouchers he'd asked for previously, plus an extra $1,200 in cash. Carroll refused the offer. His goal had moved beyond compensation to sharing his story and improving conditions for all travelers.

His newfound fame has revived his music career. His trilogy of songs about his experience has had approximately 15 million YouTube views. He's done media interviews and given speeches around the world. Ironically, the airline now uses his videos to train staff and pays him a license fee to do so, at his request.

He's also helped launch a website, Gripevine.com, for people to air problems and get them fixed. Companies now know that a disgruntled customer's view can go viral in a heartbeat and reach an immense audience. As Dave tells businesses, it's vital for companies to listen and learn.

Source: "Dave Carroll is still having problems with airlines," by Ellen Roseman, *The Toronto Star*

B Pair work Number the events in the correct order. Write *X* for the two events that are not part of Dave's story. Then take turns telling the story in your own words.

____ a. Dave decided to use his songwriting skills to address his problem in a creative way.

____ b. Dave rejected the airline's offer even though they'd doubled his original request.

____ c. Dave sued the airline for the amount of money it would cost to repair his guitar.

____ d. Dave's guitar was damaged by an airline, and they refused to compensate him.

____ e. The airline offered Dave what he wanted after he posted his song on YouTube.

____ f. Dave gave up on his dreams of becoming a musician after 20 years in the business.

____ g. Dave helped start an online consumer group and relaunched his career.

C Group work Discuss these questions. Then share your answers with the class.

1. What made Dave finally feel empowered during his struggle with the airline?
2. In what ways has social media given ordinary people more power? Give examples.

LESSON B Let's do something about it!

11 VALUES

LESSON A ▸ How honest are you?

1 STARTING POINT
What would you do?

A Look at the situations and people's responses. What would you do?

If you accidentally damaged a parked car in a parking lot . . .

"If the owner weren't around, I'd leave a note with my phone number."

"I wouldn't leave a note if the owner weren't around."

If you found out your co-worker got the job using false credentials . . .

"I would keep it a secret only if I liked my co-worker."

"I would keep it a secret unless my boss asked me directly about it."

If you found some money on the street . . .

"I wouldn't try to return it unless it were a large amount."

"Even if I were really broke, I'd give the money to the police."

B Pair work Now read these statistics. Do you find them surprising? Why or why not?

Of the people surveyed . . .

62% would never fail to report damaging a parked car even if nobody were present.

48% think it is unacceptable to use false credentials on a job application.

18% wouldn't keep money they found on the street.

58% would never illegally avoid paying the fare on public transportation.

25% think it's never OK to exceed the speed limit while driving.

Source: British Election Study at the University of Essex, Economic and Social Research Council

2 LISTENING
Finders keepers

🔊 Listen to Aaron and Leanne talking about finding something. Are these statements true or false, or does the person not say? Choose the correct answer.

	True	False	Doesn't say
1. Aaron's son wanted to keep the wallet and spend the money.	☐	☐	☐
2. Aaron's son received a thank-you card as a reward.	☐	☐	☐
3. The owner of the book probably didn't care much about it.	☐	☐	☐
4. Leanne will probably return the book.	☐	☐	☐

3 GRAMMAR

Present unreal conditional with *unless*, *only if*, and *even if*

Unless clauses include exceptions that would change the speaker's decision.
I **wouldn't** try to return it **unless** it **were** a large amount.
I **would** keep it a secret **unless** my boss **asked** me directly about it.

Only if clauses stress the condition for the result.
I **would** keep it a secret **only if** I **liked** my co-worker.

Even if clauses are followed by unexpected results.
Even if I **were** really broke, **I'd** give the money to the police.

GRAMMAR PLUS see page 126

A Look at the Starting Point on page 88 again. Look at the responses to the first situation. Are they different in meaning? If so, how?

B Choose the words that are true for you. Then complete the sentences.

1. If a cashier undercharged me, I (*would*) / *wouldn't* tell him *if* / (*even if*) . . .
   If a cashier undercharged me, I would tell him even if it were a small difference.
2. I *would* / *wouldn't* borrow a lot of money from a friend *only if* / *unless* . . .
3. I *would* / *wouldn't* return a gift I'd received to the store *if* / *unless* . . .
4. I *would* / *wouldn't* "temporarily borrow" an unlocked bicycle on the street *only if* / *even if* . . .
5. I *would* / *wouldn't* report my friend for skipping work *only if* / *unless* . . .

4 VOCABULARY & SPEAKING

It's a little unethical.

A These words describe people's ethics and attitudes. Which prefixes give them the opposite meaning? Put the words in the correct columns.

| acceptable | approving | fair | legal | rational | scrupulous |
| agreeable | ethical | honest | logical | responsible | trustworthy |

dis-	il-	ir-	un-
			unacceptable

B Pair work Use the vocabulary words in part A to discuss these questions.

1. Would you ever make an international call from work to save money?
2. Would you ever play a practical joke on your friends?
3. Would you ever tell a friend with a terrible new haircut that you think it's fantastic?

VOCABULARY PLUS see page 140

5 DISCUSSION
Ethical dilemmas

A Read these situations. What would you do?

What Would You Do?

1. You've had plans for several weeks to visit your aunt. The day before, your friend invites you to a really great party the same night.
   - Would you cancel your original plans?
   - If so, would you tell the truth or "a white lie" about why you were canceling?
   - Would you cancel your plans even if you knew your aunt were looking forward to seeing you?

2. You're at a convenience store, and you see someone shoplifting a can of soup.
   - Would you tell the clerk?
   - What if the shoplifter were a woman with a small child?
   - Would it make a difference if the shoplifter looked dangerous?

3. You work full-time during the day. You're also a part-time student in an evening course, so you have a student ID card. Businesses all over town give discounts to students.
   - Would you use your student ID to get the cheaper prices?
   - What if you earned a high salary at your job?
   - Would it make a difference if you were buying from a major chain store or from a small mom-and-pop business?

B **Group work** Share your answers and give reasons for each. Then agree on the best course of action for each situation.

"Unless it were a special occasion for my aunt, I might leave a little early so I could get to the party before it ended."

6 DISCUSSION
Too good to be true

A Which of these situations seem reliable? Choose those that seem legitimate.

- [ ] 1. A website offers free international phone service.
- [ ] 2. A company sends you an email asking you to confirm your credit card details online.
- [ ] 3. Someone on the street asks you to sign a petition that requires your address and phone number.
- [ ] 4. A television ad offers a set of knives worth $300 for just $75.

B **Pair work** Discuss these or similar situations. Share your own experiences or those of people you know.

"I once bought a kitchen appliance that I saw advertised on TV. The price was really good, and it worked well at first, but after a few weeks, it broke."

7 WRITING
Thesis statements

> A topic sentence states the main idea of a single paragraph. A thesis statement introduces the topic of a composition. It is often located at the beginning or end of the first paragraph.

A Read the composition and choose the best thesis statement from the choices below. Then, write a *T* where you think the thesis statement should appear.

1. I've made some bad decisions.
2. We learn a lot from the decisions we make.
3. I have good and bad memories of old friendships.

When I'm faced with a decision that puts my ethics on the line, I think about what similar situations in the past have taught me. In my life, I've made both good and bad choices.

One of my good decisions resulted in a casual friend becoming a very close friend. A college classmate gave me a lottery ticket for my birthday. As she gave it to me, she joked that if I won, I should split the prize with her. I ended up winning $500. At the time, I was saving for a new tablet, and with the $500, I had enough money. I considered not telling my friend that I'd won. But I felt dishonest and disloyal, and I gave her half. I'll always be glad I did, and I wouldn't do it any differently today, even if I really needed all the money. Today, she is still one of my best friends.

One of my bad decisions ruined a friendship. A former classmate wanted a job with my company and asked me to recommend her. I knew she didn't have very good work habits. I told her I would do it only if she promised to work hard. She was hired, but three months later, she was fired because my boss thought she was irresponsible and her work was unacceptable. I was fairly new at the company myself, and my company is still a little unsure about trusting my judgment now. I don't have much to do with her these days.

I believe that good and bad decisions are a part of everyone's personal development. Is it possible to learn from those experiences? I think it is because even the bad ones help to prepare you for the future.

B Write a four-paragraph composition about a happy memory or a regret. Follow these guidelines.

1st paragraph: Introduce your topic in the paragraph. Begin or end the paragraph with your thesis statement.

2nd paragraph: Write about a decision you would make again.

3rd paragraph: Write about a decision you would make differently.

4th paragraph: End with a strong conclusion.

Your thesis statement . . .
- should contain a *single* idea.
- should be neither too *general* nor too *specific*.
- should unify all the *paragraphs*.
- can be *improved* as you write.

C **Group work** Take turns reading your compositions. Is the thesis statement too general? Does it need to be improved?

LESSON B ▸ Taking stock

1 STARTING POINT
I wish . . .

A Read these messages. Match each message with one of the values below.

a. careful spending   c. perseverance   e. career advancement
b. concern for others   d. good family relations f. good cross-cultural relations

The Connected World

Today's questions: I've had so many cool friends in my life. I wish I'd stayed in touch with all of them! Is there anything you wish you'd done differently? What do you wish you could change right now?

____ **1. Mika22** — I wish I had enough nerve to ask for a promotion. I like my job, but I've been in the same position for several years. If only my boss would consider promoting me!

____ **2. Ivan007** — I love and respect my mother and father a lot. I wish I hadn't given them such a hard time when I was growing up. I'm just happy they forgave me for all those rough times.

____ **3. Wishful** — I'm ashamed of all the money I've wasted. If only I'd saved more over the last few years. Now I want to rent my own apartment, and I can't afford to! Starting today, I'm going to stop buying things I don't need.

____ **4. JackD** — I used to travel to Mexico for my job about once a month. I probably would have been more successful if I had spoken more Spanish. I wish I'd taken a few Spanish classes.

____ **5. SportsFan** — When I was a kid, I tried lots of things – sports, languages, music – and I enjoyed them all, but I always lost interest after a while. If I had stuck with something, I could have gotten good at it.

____ **6. Ruby65** — I wish I could find the time to do volunteer work. I feel I'm not contributing enough to the community. Maybe I can find time to volunteer at the hospital in my neighborhood.

B **Pair work** Which person in part A are you most like? Which of the values are the most important? What are some of the values you learned when you were growing up?

"I'm similar to Ruby65. I really think it's important to show concern for other people. As I was growing up, my parents also taught me the importance of . . ."

2 GRAMMAR

Wishes and regrets

For wishes about the present and future, use *wish* + simple past, past continuous, or *could* / *would* + verb.
I **wish** I **had** enough nerve to ask for a promotion.
I **wish** I **could find** the time to do volunteer work.

For regrets about the past, use *wish* + past perfect.
I **wish** I'**d taken** a few Spanish classes.
I **wish** I **hadn't given** my parents such a hard time when I was growing up.

For regrets about the past, use *if* + past perfect and *could* / *would have* + past participle.
If I **had stuck** with something, I **could have gotten** good at it.

For strong wishes about the present or future, or for strong regrets about the past, use *if only*.
If only clauses are often used without a main clause.
If only my boss **would consider** promoting me!

GRAMMAR PLUS see page 127

A Look at the Starting Point on page 92 again. Which sentences express regrets about the past? Which ones describe wishes for the present or future?

B Rewrite these statements using the words in parentheses. Compare answers with a partner. Are any of the sentences true for you?

1. I can't find the time to exercise. (I wish . . .)
   I wish I could find the time to exercise.
2. My grades weren't very good last semester. (If only . . .)
3. I don't know how to dance very well. (I wish . . .)
4. I didn't apply for that interesting job at work. (I wish . . .)
5. I'm feeling very stressed these days. (I wish . . .)
6. I never learned how to swim when I was a child. (If only . . .)
7. I gave away my old guitar last year. (If only . . .)
8. I watched too much TV and didn't read enough when I was a kid. (If only . . .)

C Complete these sentences with your own wishes or regrets and add extra information. Then compare answers with a partner.

1. If only I had enough money to . . . ! Then I wouldn't . . .
   If only I had enough money to buy a motorcycle!
   Then I wouldn't have to take the bus to class.
2. I wish I could find the time to . . . . If I could, I would . . .
3. I wish I had learned how to . . . when I was a kid. If I had, I'd . . .
4. If only I knew how to . . . . Then I could . . .
5. I wish my friends would . . . so that . . .
6. If only I had listened to my parents when they told me . . . because . . .
7. I wish they would pass a law that says . . . . If they did, . . .
8. If only I had the courage to . . . . Then I would . . .

LESSON B Taking stock

3 VOCABULARY & SPEAKING
Personal values

A What words describe people's values? Complete the chart with the correct noun or adjective.

Noun	Adjective	Noun	Adjective	Noun	Adjective
compassion	compassionate		indifferent	selfishness	
	discreet	kindness		sensitivity	
generosity		resilience			tender
	honest		respectful		tolerant

B Pair work Which three values do you think are most important? Decide with a partner. Give your reasons.

"We thought generosity, tolerance, and honesty were most important. Generosity is an important value because if you help people, they might help you one day. Tolerance matters because . . ."

VOCABULARY PLUS see page 140

4 LISTENING & SPEAKING
Three important values

A Listen to these on-the-street interviews. What values do these people think are important? Number the values in the order you hear them.

___ honesty   ___ privacy   ___ respect

B Listen again. Whose answer did you agree with the most? Why do you think so?

"I'd say I agreed with the first woman the most. If you're not honest, you'll only get yourself into trouble. Plus, telling the truth is the right thing to do."

5 SPEAKING
Grant me a wish.

A If you could have three wishes, what would they be? Make a list.

B Pair work Compare your wishes with a partner. Then share your answers with the class.

"My first wish would be for my family to stay healthy and happy. Second, I would wish for more peace in the world. For my last wish, . . ."

6 READING

Subway Superman

A **Pair work** Read the title and the first paragraph of the news article. What would you have done if you were Wesley Autrey? Discuss, and then read the article.

NEW YORK HONORS A HERO

It started as a typical day for Wesley Autrey, a 50-year-old construction worker in New York City. It was about 12:45 P.M., and he was waiting on a subway platform to take his daughters home before he went to work. He suddenly noticed a man nearby have convulsions and collapse. Mr. Autrey and two women went to help the stranger. The man, Cameron Hollopeter, managed to get to his feet, but then stumbled at the edge of the platform and fell onto the subway tracks. Mr. Autrey looked up and saw the lights of the subway train approaching through the tunnel.

What would you do? Stand horrified and watch helplessly? Most people would jump in to help, but only if there were no train in sight. Mr. Autrey acted quickly. He leapt down onto the track. He realized that he didn't have time to get Mr. Hollopeter and himself back up on the platform before the train arrived, so he lay on top of the man and pressed down as hard as he could. Although the driver tried to stop the train before it reached them, he couldn't. Five cars passed over them before the train finally stopped. The cars had passed only inches from his head. His first words were to ask the onlookers to tell his daughters he was OK.

New York loves a hero. And there was no question that Mr. Autrey's actions had been just that – heroic. He became an overnight sensation. People couldn't get enough of the story. The media named him the "Subway Superman." New York City Mayor Michael Bloomberg gave him the Bronze Medallion, the city's highest honor. (In the past, this honor has gone to such people as General Douglas MacArthur, Martin Luther King Jr., and Muhammad Ali.) Mr. Autrey was also asked to appear on several high-profile television talk shows.

His selfless bravery was also rewarded with money and gifts. Among other things, Mr. Autrey received: $10,000 from Donald Trump, a $5,000 gift card from the Gap clothing store, a new Jeep, tickets and backstage passes to a Beyoncé concert, and a free one-year public transit pass. A "Disney ambassador" thanked him with a one-week all-expenses-paid trip to Disney World and tickets to see *The Lion King* on Broadway.

How did Autrey, a Navy veteran, react to all this? Honorably. He said, "I don't feel like I did anything spectacular; I just saw someone who needed help. I did what I felt was right."

B Read the article again. Are these statements true or false? Choose the correct answer. Correct the false statements.

	True	False
1. Autrey hadn't noticed Hollopeter before he fell onto the tracks.	☐	☐
2. There was very little space between Autrey and the bottom of the train.	☐	☐
3. Autrey jumped onto the tracks because he wanted to be a hero.	☐	☐

C **Group work** Discuss these questions.

1. Have you ever had the opportunity to help someone in trouble or in danger?
2. Why do you think so many businesses wanted to reward Mr. Autrey?

12 MOVING AROUND
LESSON A ▶ Culture shock

1 STARTING POINT
The benefits of studying abroad

A Read this website. Choose three benefits of studying a language abroad that you feel are the most important.

LTI LANGUAGE TRAVELERS INSTITUTE

OPENING DOORS TO THE WORLD
Study Abroad with Language Travelers Institute!

Consider enrolling in one of LTI's affordable programs of language study abroad. Then imagine yourself by the end of next year:
- You will have been studying your chosen language for 12 months.
- You will have been interacting with people from other cultures, which will have changed the way you view the world.
- You will have been living in a fascinating foreign land.

And, if you're like over 90% of LTI's former students, by this time next year:
- Your self-confidence will have increased.
- Your commitment to language study will have gotten stronger.
- You will have made many fascinating new friends!

Study abroad with Language Travelers Institute and the world will become your oyster.

LTI SCHOOLS | STUDY ABROAD | CONTACT US

B Pair work Discuss your choices. What are some other benefits of studying or living abroad?

"I think interacting with people from other cultures is the most important benefit."

2 VOCABULARY & SPEAKING
Words of encouragement

A Complete these verbs and phrases with a preposition from the box.

| about | in | of | to | with |

1. adjust _to_
2. be excited _____
3. be scared _____
4. be familiar _____
5. become aware _____
6. get accustomed _____
7. look forward _____
8. participate _____
9. take advantage _____

B Pair work What challenges do people face when they live or study abroad? Discuss with a partner using the verbs and phrases in part A.

"Sometimes people are scared of starting a new job abroad because they aren't familiar with the routines."

VOCABULARY PLUS see page 141

3 GRAMMAR

Future perfect and future perfect continuous

Use the future perfect to emphasize that something will be completed or achieved by a particular point in the future.
By this time next year, your self-confidence **will have increased**.

Use the future perfect continuous to emphasize the duration of an activity in progress at a particular point in the future.
By the end of next year, you **will have been studying** your chosen language for 12 months.

GRAMMAR PLUS see page 128

A Look at the Starting Point on page 96 again. Can you find more examples of the future perfect and the future perfect continuous?

B These sentences about Joon's year abroad all have mistakes. Correct the mistakes using the future with *will*, the future perfect, or the future perfect continuous. Then compare answers with a partner.

1. By this time tomorrow, Joon ~~will travel~~ *will have been traveling* for 24 hours.

2. By the end of next week, he will have been receiving his student ID card and registered for classes.

3. He'll be going out more after a few weeks because he will have been more familiar with the city.

4. After studying English for a few months, he will have felt more confident about speaking to people.

5. By this time next year, his younger sister will have been visiting him once or twice. When she's older, she probably will have wanted to study abroad, too.

6. I'm sure he will change a lot by the time he comes back to Korea.

7. His family will have been surprised when he gets back because he will have been changing so much.

8. And just think – the next time we see him, Joon will turn 22 already, and he will be away for a year!

C Use these time expressions to write sentences using the future perfect or future perfect continuous. Then share them with a partner.

1. Before this class ends, . . .
2. By the end of the day, . . .
3. By the end of the week, . . .
4. At the end of the year, . . .
5. In two years' time, . . .
6. By the year 2030, . . .

LESSON A Culture shock

4 DISCUSSION
Customs and traditions

A Read this list of Canadian customs. Are they the same as or different from those where you live? Choose the correct answer.

		Same	Different
01	Both men and women shake hands with each other when they meet.	☐	☐
02	Business meetings are friendly, but there isn't much socializing beforehand.	☐	☐
03	Lunch is usually a fairly light meal that doesn't last long.	☐	☐
04	People are usually punctual for business appointments.	☐	☐
05	It's common to ask people you meet what kind of work they do.	☐	☐
06	Many people eat dinner early in the evening, around 6:00 P.M.	☐	☐
07	At the dinner table, the fork is generally held in the left hand and the knife in the right.	☐	☐
08	People offer to take their shoes off when entering somebody's home.	☐	☐
09	When invited to someone's home, a gift, such as flowers or dessert, is usually expected.	☐	☐
10	Most people open gifts as soon as they receive them.	☐	☐

B *Group work* How do you feel about the customs in part A? Explain your opinions.

"I think women should kiss on the cheek when they meet. Just shaking hands seems kind of cold somehow."

5 LISTENING
When in Rome . . .

A Listen to Andrew, Rachel, and Layla talking about their experiences abroad. Answer the questions.

1. What helped each of them get used to their new living situation?
2. What did each person find difficult to adjust to?

B Listen again. Did Andrew (*A*), Rachel (*R*), or Layla (*L*) do these things? Write the correct letter.

____ 1. felt homesick
____ 2. had fun playing a sport
____ 3. enjoyed food with friends
____ 4. didn't feel connected to others at first
____ 5. ate dinner late at night
____ 6. thought people talked about themselves too much
____ 7. enjoyed the old buildings
____ 8. watched comedy shows on TV
____ 9. tried to talk about herself

6 WRITING
Conclusions

> The conclusion can close your composition by restating the main idea, summarizing the main points, looking to the future, making recommendations, or a combination of these methods.

A Read these two concluding paragraphs. Which methods do the writers use? Underline the parts of the conclusions that helped you decide.

> Overall, for the majority of young people, taking a year off to travel has not replaced the traditional postsecondary pursuit of higher education. For most high school graduates, studying or training for a career will remain the most likely path. However, there are still many young people who save as much money as they can in order to see foreign sights and experience foreign cultures. Taking time to travel may put them behind a year as far as college and careers are concerned, but they say the personal growth is worth it.

> In brief, there are real benefits to studying abroad. While it is certainly possible to learn the language in a country where it is not widely spoken, living abroad offers limitless possibilities for improvement. Additionally, foreign students have a real opportunity to hone their life skills. Generally, they are responsible for everything from money management, accommodations, and meals to ensuring that they have a good balance between their social life and school life. Studying abroad offers not only language lessons, but also life lessons, and is well worth considering.

B Find these linking words or phrases in the conclusions. How are they used? Do you know any others that have similar meanings?

> additionally   generally   however   in brief   overall

C Write a composition about living or traveling abroad. Choose one of these topics or one of your own. Your conclusion should use at least one of the methods described and some linking words or phrases.

- culture shock
- group travel
- independent travel
- studying abroad

D Pair work Exchange papers with a partner and answer these questions.

1. What methods did your partner use in his or her conclusion?
2. Are the linking words used effectively? Why or why not?
3. Can you offer any suggestions to improve your partner's conclusion?

LESSON B ▸ Traveler or tourist?

1 STARTING POINT
Travel tips

A Read these people's experiences and the expert's advice. Can you think of any other advice?

TERRY'S Travel Tips

Get advice from Terry Tripper, the travel expert, and share your own travel tips.

Meg B. says: A woman fell down in front of me during a sightseeing tour. I helped her up, but soon after, I couldn't find my wallet. Do you think she might have taken it?

Terry says: It's very likely. If you hadn't been so nice, you would probably still have your wallet. It's a common scam – someone pretends to be in trouble, but actually turns out to be a thief!

Bruno H. says: I want to share a tip my friend gave me that I used on my last vacation. If you're worried about losing your passport, like I am, don't carry it around with you. Just keep it in your hotel room.

Terry says: That is a good tip if there is a safe in your room. If not, keep your passport with you at all times. If someone had broken into your room, you would probably still be trying to get home!

Kim N. says: On my last trip abroad, I brought a little notebook and pen to help me communicate while shopping. If I couldn't find something, I'd draw a picture. If I hadn't had that notebook and pen, my friends wouldn't be thanking me for the awesome souvenirs I brought them!

Terry says: That's a great idea! When phrasebooks and dictionaries don't help, a picture can be worth a thousand words. But you know there are also some great apps for that, right? Check out this website.

B Pair work What travel questions would you ask Terry? Tell your partner. Then try to offer advice to each other.

"I want to buy souvenirs from the places I'm going to visit, but I also like to travel light. Should I store them at the airport or somewhere else?"

"The best thing would be to mail them home. If you don't mind waiting, use surface mail instead of airmail. It's cheaper."

2 LISTENING
Things went wrong.

A Listen to Cindy and Scott talking about their travel problems. What happened to each person?

B Listen again. Choose the statements you think are probably true. Compare your answers with a partner. Give reasons.

☐ 1. Cindy has a unique, easy-to-see name tag on her luggage.
☐ 2. Cindy travels frequently.
☐ 3. Scott likes peace and quiet when he travels.
☐ 4. Scott slept soundly all the way to Panama City.

3 GRAMMAR

Mixed conditionals

Use **had / hadn't** + past participle and **would / wouldn't** to talk about hypothetical events in the past that have effects on the present.
If you **hadn't been** so nice, you **would** probably still **have** your wallet!
If someone **had broken into** your room, you **would** probably still **be trying** to get home!

GRAMMAR PLUS see page 129

A Look at the Starting Point on page 100 again. Find another mixed conditional sentence. Does this sentence describe actual or hypothetical events?

B Complete these sentences with the correct form of the verbs in parentheses.

1. If I ____had been____ (be) more adventurous when I was younger, I ____wouldn't have____ (not have) any regrets about the things I missed.

2. The airline lost my luggage. If I _____ (bring) a change of clothes in my carry-on bag, I _____ (not shop) for new clothes now.

3. This flight is so long! If I _____ (not buy) an economy ticket, I _____ (be) more comfortable now.

4. If you _____ (learn) to speak some Mandarin before moving to Taipei, you _____ (be able to) ask someone for directions now.

5. If Martha _____ (not become) a flight attendant, she probably _____ (not travel) as much as she does.

4 DISCUSSION

Your own trip

A Pair work Have you ever had problems on vacation? Tell your partner. Use the topics below or your own ideas.

- health
- accommodations
- food
- safety
- language
- getting around
- costs
- weather

"I went to the beach last week, but the weather was awful."
"Why? Was it rainy?"
"No, it was too sunny. If it hadn't been so sunny, I wouldn't have this terrible sunburn now."

B Group work Share your bad travel experiences. Get advice about what you could have done differently.

LESSON B Traveler or tourist?

5 VOCABULARY
One word or two?

A Combine the items from the boxes to make compound adjectives.

culturally	assured	hearted	motivated
non	aware	judgmental	reliant
open	conforming	minded	sensitive
self			

culturally aware, nonjudgmental, open-minded, . . .

B Pair work Are the characteristics in part A important when you travel? Give an example for each one.

"If you're culturally aware, you'll find it easier to accept cultural differences."

VOCABULARY PLUS see page 141

6 ROLE PLAY
Planning a trip

A Group work Imagine you are planning a vacation. Discuss these questions. Write notes about what your group decides for each question.

1. Where would you like to go?
2. How long would you like your stay to last?
3. Would you like to go with a tour group or on your own?
4. What type of accommodations do you prefer?
5. What kinds of activities would you like to do during the day?
6. What sorts of evening activities would you prefer?
7. What would each person's budget be?
8. What types of transportation would you plan on using?

B Class activity Choose someone in your group to act as a travel agent and present your vacation to the class. The class votes on the best itinerary.

"We have planned a truly exotic vacation for you in the remote Galápagos Islands! You'll stay for seven unforgettable days in a five-star resort . . ."

UNIT 12 Moving around

7 READING
Solo travel

A What are the best ways to experience a new place when you travel? Make a list. Then read the article to compare your list with the author's.

Get Yourself LOST

Travelers to a new city are often encouraged to take a bus tour. The thinking is that they can later return to the places that **captivated** them, but that's nonsense! What you see from the inside of a fast-moving bus is sanitized and unreal, utterly removed from the authentic sights, sounds, and smells outside.

The best way to experience any destination is by foot, without an itinerary, wandering where your spirit leads you. Even in the largest cities, the **savvy** traveler **plunges** into the very center of town and walks down the nearest street, experiencing the actual life of the people while looking into the grocery stores and courtyards. You eventually get to many of the same sites that are on the bus route – the museums, the monuments, the city hall – but you will have witnessed so much more because you will have felt the contemporary life of the city you're visiting.

"But what if I get lost?" people ask. No one ever gets permanently lost in a major city. Eventually, a trolley or bus passes with the words "Central Station" on its front and you can easily return to the center of town. Besides, the most wonderful things can happen if you do get lost, such as stopping at a sidewalk café to sit and relax and then asking directions from the locals at the next table. Hopefully, your trip may be **enhanced** by this encounter. Here are a few ways to make the most of your travels:

▸ **KNOW BEFORE YOU GO.** Before you depart, spend time learning about the history and culture of your destination so you will better understand the place you're visiting.

▸ **MOVE AROUND LIKE A LOCAL.** Use the local subways, trams, and buses. You'll not only save money, you'll learn how people live there, and you'll gain a realistic perspective of the city.

▸ **CHECK THE BULLETIN BOARDS.** Bulletin boards list free lectures, concerts, workshops, and social gatherings, giving you a chance to join or meet the area's most **dynamic** residents.

▸ **TAKE A WALKING TOUR.** If you must book a guided tour, select the nonstandard, inexpensive kinds conducted on foot.

So, the next time you feel lured by a sightseeing bus tour, save your money and instead, wander around on your own. I promise you a time you'll remember fondly.

Source: "Get Yourself Lost," by Arthur Frommer

B Find the boldfaced words in the article. Then choose the correct words to complete the sentences.

1. If something **captivates** you, you're *upset / captured / delighted* by it.
2. A **savvy** traveler is *refined / experienced / adventurous*.
3. When you **plunge** into an activity, you probably *walk away from it / throw yourself into it / stumble into it*.
4. If you **enhance** your reading skills, you *upgrade / restore / prolong* them.
5. **Dynamic** people are more *cautious / unstable / interesting* than others.

C Pair work How do your travel habits compare with those in the article? Which ideas do you think you'll try the next time you visit a new city? Why?

LESSON B Traveler or tourist?

COMMUNICATION REVIEW
UNITS 10–12

✓ SELF-ASSESSMENT

How well can you do these things? Choose the best answer.

I can . . .	Very well	OK	A little
▸ Describe annoying behavior (Ex. 1)	☐	☐	☐
▸ Make and respond to customer complaints (Ex. 1)	☐	☐	☐
▸ Discuss hypothetical situations in my present and future life (Ex. 2)	☐	☐	☐
▸ Understand the main points of a training workshop about customer service (Ex. 3)	☐	☐	☐
▸ Express and explain my opinions in a discussion about living and working in a different culture (Ex. 4)	☐	☐	☐
▸ Make hypotheses about past and present events in my life (Ex. 5)	☐	☐	☐

Now do the corresponding exercises. Was your assessment correct?

1 ROLE PLAY
Annoying customers

A What do you think annoys these people about their passengers or customers?

1. bus drivers
2. flight attendants
3. tech support workers
4. waiters/waitresses

"Something that probably makes bus drivers crazy is when people complain that the buses are running late. It usually isn't the drivers' fault."

B Pair work Take turns playing the role of a customer complaining and an employee responding to the complaints.

2 DISCUSSION
I'd like to try . . .

A Look at these questions and write answers that are true for you.

1. What is something you'd like to try, even if it were a little risky?
2. What is something you would do only if it were a matter of life or death?
3. Where is someplace you wouldn't want to go unless someone went with you?

B Pair work Discuss your answers with a partner.

"I'd like to try scuba diving at night, even if it were a little risky. I think diving in the ocean at night must be incredible."

3 LISTENING
Training

🔊 **A** Listen to a training workshop. What job are the trainees going to do?

🔊 **B** Listen again. Are these statements true or false? Choose the correct answer.

	True	False
1. Sammy would try to get the customer on a flight the same day.	☐	☐
2. Andrea says the customer should have left more time between flights.	☐	☐
3. Ricardo says the customer should be ashamed for being late.	☐	☐
4. Hannah would direct the customer to a place where she could get refreshed.	☐	☐

4 DISCUSSION
Culture shock

A **Pair work** How important are these personality traits for someone who is living and working in a new culture? Number them from 1 to 6 (1 = most important, 6 = least important).

It's important to be . . .

☐ culturally aware   ☐ nonjudgmental
☐ open-minded   ☐ self-assured
☐ self-aware   ☐ self-reliant

B **Group work** Join another pair. Explain your rankings to the group and discuss any differences of opinion.

5 DISCUSSION
What if . . . ?

A **Pair work** Discuss the questions.

How would your life be different today if . . .
1. you'd been born in another country?
2. you'd grown up in a much smaller or larger family?
3. you hadn't learned any English?
4. you hadn't met your best friend?

B **Group work** What event or circumstance has had the biggest effect on you? How would your life be different if that event hadn't happened?

"I think growing up in an extended family had the biggest effect on me. If my grandmother hadn't been living with us, I wouldn't have such an awareness of my culture and my ancestors."

GRAMMAR PLUS

1A Verbs followed by gerunds

These verbs are followed by a gerund.
deny   discuss   finish   mention   practice   quit   resist   suggest

These verbs are followed by an infinitive.
arrange   claim   decide   demand   deserve   expect   pretend   refuse   volunteer

Some common expressions are always followed by gerunds.
She **had fun / a good time** arranging the party.
He **has trouble / a tough time** getting his assignments in on time.
He**'s busy** cooking dinner right now.
She never **worries about** cleaning up after herself.

Some verbs take either a gerund or an infinitive, but the meaning of the sentence will be different.
I **stopped to drink** some coffee. *(I ended one activity and began another.)*
I **stopped drinking** coffee. *(I don't do that activity anymore.)*
I **stopped running** when I got tired. *(I temporarily ended the activity.)*

1 Complete these sentences with the gerund or infinitive form of the verb in parentheses.

1. I practiced ___*speaking*___ (speak) English with an American friend last night.
2. He volunteered _____ (help) at the hospital fund-raiser.
3. They discussed _____ (go) somewhere exotic on their vacation this year.
4. She's stopped _____ (talk) to him because they had a big argument.
5. My great-grandmother has trouble _____ (get) to our family reunions.
6. Laura always denies _____ (be) wild and crazy, but she really is.

2 Choose the best answer to complete the sentences.

My friend Shanda is pretty cool and very outgoing. She's usually busy (1) *to do /* (*doing*) a million things at once. Last week, I suggested (2) *to go / going* out for dinner and (3) *to see / seeing* a movie. We arranged (4) *to meet / meeting* at 7:00. Well, I know she doesn't worry about (5) *to be / being* on time, but she didn't show up until 7:30. At first, she said it took her a long time to finish (6) *to get / getting* ready. Then, after the movie, she couldn't resist (7) *to tell / telling* me what really happened. She was having such a good time (8) *to play / playing* video games with her brother that she forgot about our plans. It's a good thing I'm the laid-back type!

1B Noun clauses after *be*

The downside of, the upside of, the hard part about, the good thing about, the only thing about, the trick to, the secret to, and *one difficulty with* are used in complex phrases that introduce noun clauses after *be*.
The downside of sharing a bedroom is (that) it's hard to have any privacy.
The hard part about being a twin is (that) people are always calling you by the wrong name.
The trick to living in a crowded house is (that) you have to find a private space of your own.
One difficulty with being the youngest is (that) everyone is always telling you what to do.

The phrases ending with a preposition can be followed by a gerund phrase, *not* + a gerund phrase, or a noun phrase.
The secret to **getting along with your siblings** is (that) you have to respect their privacy.
The good thing about **not being in a big family** is (that) you always get to choose what's on TV.
The upside of **a large family** is (that) you always have someone to spend time with.
The only thing about **working moms** is (that) they have less time to spend with you.

1 Complete the sentences with *about*, *of*, *with*, or *to*.

1. The best thing ____*about*____ my grandmother living with us is that she's a great cook.

2. The upside _____ being a two-income family is we can afford a few small luxuries.

3. One difficulty _____ living with my in-laws is that they want everything their way.

4. The trick _____ living in a large family is you have to learn to respect each other.

5. The hard part _____ strict parents is you always have to remember the rules.

6. The problem _____ not going to our family reunion is I won't see my cousins.

2 Rewrite the sentences. Change the noun phrases in boldface to gerund phrases.

1. The trouble with **a big family** is it's expensive to feed everyone.
   The trouble with having a big family is it's expensive to feed everyone.

2. The trick to **a two-income family** is you have to schedule family time together.

3. The hard part about **a big house** is there's so much work to do.

4. The upside of **a big house** is no one has to share a room.

5. The only bad thing about **little brothers** is I always have to babysit them.

6. One good thing about **little sisters** is they really look up to you.

7. One problem with **an extended family** is we had to get a bigger car.

8. The greatest thing about **a small house** is the bills are a lot lower.

2A Past modals and phrasal modals of obligation

Some past modals and phrasal modals of obligation are stronger than others.

Strong obligation: To show that there was no choice about doing the action, use *had to*.
(Note that *must* is not used in the past.)
My parents **had to** go to school on Saturdays.

Expectation: There was a general expectation that an action was required or prohibited.
She **was supposed to** talk to her professor after class. *(But she probably didn't.)*
He **wasn't supposed to** drive the car to school. *(But he probably did.)*

Advisability: There was a good idea or a correct action in a particular situation, but it was or was not done.
He **should have** taken better notes in class. *(But he didn't.)*
She **shouldn't have** bought such an expensive jacket. *(But she did.)*

Necessity: The action was considered to be necessary or unnecessary. However, unlike *had to*, there is a choice about doing or not doing the action.
I **needed to** make an appointment with the counselor.
I **didn't need to** buy the textbook, but I thought it looked interesting.

No obligation: There is complete choice about doing the action.
I **didn't have to** take piano lessons, but I wanted to.

---

1 Choose the correct answer to complete the sentence.

1. Jan *should have* / (*shouldn't have*) ignored the problem because it only got worse.
2. I *was supposed to* / *didn't have to* go on vacation, but I didn't save enough money.
3. Yoko *needed to* / *wasn't supposed to* ignore her parents' advice, but she did.
4. He fixed the leak himself, so he *didn't need to call* / *should have called* a plumber.
5. When I got older, I *had to* / *wasn't supposed to* learn to solve my own problems.
6. I *needed to* / *didn't have to* book my flight so early, but I wanted a good seat.

2 Complete the sentences with *(not) had to*, *was (not) supposed to*, *should (not) have*, or *(not) needed to* and the correct form of the verb in parentheses. Sometimes more than one answer is possible.

1. A: I heard Rob's cell phone rang in the middle of the test. What happened?
   B: He __had to leave__ (leave) the room immediately and was given a failing grade.

2. A: You're home early, Jenny. I thought your English exam lasted until 4:00.
   B: I finished early, and the teacher said I _____ (stay) if I didn't want to.

3. A: Have you seen Steven this morning? He's late for the test.
   B: No, I haven't. He _____ (meet) me for breakfast, but he didn't show up.

4. A: The teacher recommends using a pencil on tests so you can erase wrong answers.
   B: Yes, and I _____ (follow) his advice. I made a real mess with my pen.

2B Modals with multiple uses

Degrees of certainty range from very certain to uncertain.

Very certain: To show that you think something was probable in the past, use *must have*, *must not have*, *can't have*, or *couldn't have*.
Jake had a stomachache last night after dinner. He **must have** eaten too much.
Sofia was at a movie with me last night. You **couldn't have** seen her at the mall!

Uncertain: To show that you think something was possible in the past, use *could have*, *may have*, *might have*, *may not have*, or *might not have*.
Jun Ho is usually here by now. He **could / may / might have** missed the bus this morning.
Tanya was supposed to meet me before school. She **may / might not have** gotten the message.

To give opinions or advice, there are a greater number of modals available for talking about the present or future than there are for the past.

Present or future: Use *must (not)*, *have to*, *have got to*, *had better (not)*, or *should (not)*.
Parents **have got to** monitor the shows their children watch.
The kids **had better not** spend so much time indoors playing computer games.

Past: Use *should (not) have*.
I **should have** listened to the advice my parents gave me about having a healthy lifestyle.
We **should not have** ignored the scientists' warnings about global warming.

Choose the correct answer to complete the sentence.

1. A: Kimberly didn't come to the party last night. I wonder why.
   B: I'm not sure. She (could have) / *should have* been sick, I guess.

2. A: Where's my umbrella? It was right here by the door.
   B: Oh, I'm sorry, Paul. My sister *couldn't have / must have* taken it.

3. A: I got a terrible cramp in my leg while I was jogging yesterday.
   B: Hmm. You *must not have / may have* done your stretches properly first.

4. A: I had to ask Natalie twice to turn down the TV.
   B: She *might not have / must have* heard you the first time.

5. A: They said the meeting was at 7:30, but it had already started when I got there.
   B: They told me 7:00. You *can't have / must have* been told the wrong time.

6. A: Marnie wasn't at work yesterday. Was she sick?
   B: Well, she *couldn't have / must have* been too sick. I saw her at the park.

7. A: I only used your camera to take a few pictures. I don't see why you're so upset.
   B: Well, you *couldn't have / shouldn't have* been using it without my permission.

8. A: Sorry I'm late. We were playing baseball, and I didn't notice the time.
   B: You *may not have / couldn't have* been doing that. It's been dark for an hour!

3A Defining and non-defining relative clauses

That can be used for people or things in defining relative clauses. However, it cannot be used as a replacement for *where* or *when* with the meaning "in which," "at which," or "during which."
Many of the people **that live in Paris** leave the city in August to vacation in other places.
A statue of ducks **that can be found in Boston** is a popular tourist attraction for children.
Pamplona is that city in Spain **where the bulls run through the streets during a summer festival**.
Summer is the season **when New York is crowded with tourists from all over the world**.

That cannot be used in non-defining relative clauses. *Who*, *which*, or *where* are used instead.
Cairo, **which has fascinated Europeans for ages**, draws countless tourists each year.
Our tour guide, **who knew a great deal about souvenirs in Otavalo**, helped us buy some beautiful presents for our friends.

1 Complete the defining relative clauses with *that*, *who*, *when*, or *where*. Sometimes more than one answer is possible.

1. People __who / that__ live in cities have more stress than people _____ live in small towns.
2. Amy likes to stay in hotels _____ there are lots of theaters and restaurants nearby.
3. Some city people have cottages by lakes _____ they can swim and relax during the summer season.
4. My family and I always visit Brazil in the month _____ the Carnaval festival begins.
5. Many office workers like to have lunch in a park _____ they can sit in the sun and enjoy the nature _____ is all around them.
6. The city is better for students _____ want to work in the summer because it's the place _____ the job market offers the most opportunities.
7. People _____ live in towns _____ there is no public transportation system often own cars.
8. If you're going to Asia in April, Tokyo is a city _____ I recommend visiting because spring is the season _____ the cherry trees are in bloom.

2 Match the information about these cities. Then make sentences with non-defining relative clauses.

1. New Yorkers / huge baseball fans __c__
2. Saint Petersburg / the Hermitage is located ____
3. Athens / 2004 Summer Olympics were held ____
4. Sydney / famous for its Opera House ____
5. Venice / built on 118 small islands ____
6. Hawaii / has warm weather all year ____

a. was also the location of the first games.
b. is a popular winter destination.
c. have two pro teams in their city.
d. is crossed by many canals.
e. was Russia's capital for many years.
f. also has a well-known bridge.

New Yorkers, who are huge baseball fans, have two pro teams in their city.

3B Order of modifiers

Shape (*round*, *thin*), color (*red*, *blue*), and material (*silk*, *plastic*) are also used to describe nouns. They appear in the following order:

Quality	Size	Shape	Age	Color	Type	Material	Noun
quaint	little	winding					streets
picturesque			old	brightly colored	resort		hotels
	small				Thai	wooden	fishing boats

1 Put the words in the correct order.

1. He bought a *red / house / brick / little* in the center of town.
   He bought a little red brick house in the center of town.

2. They're renting a *cottage / pink / traditional / square* beside the river.

3. He hated living in a *border / town / remote / little* with its *wooden / houses / run-down*.

4. The town had many *old / buildings / cement* with *steel / dirty / black / roofs*.

3B Connecting contrasting ideas

There are three ways to connect contrasting ideas.

To begin an adverb clause, use *although* or *even though*.
I'd like to live in a small town someday **even though** I love all the opportunities in big cities.
Although I love all the opportunities in big cities, I'd like to live in a small town someday.

To begin an independent clause, use the transition words *however*, *nevertheless*, or *on the other hand*. Note the punctuation with transition words.
I love big cities. **However** / **On the other hand**, I'd like to live in a small town someday.
I love big cities; **nevertheless** / **however**, I'd like to live in a small town someday.

To begin a noun phrase, use the prepositions *despite* or *in spite of*.
Despite all the opportunities in big cities, I'd like to live in a small town someday.
I'd like to live in a small town someday **in spite of** all the opportunities in big cities.

2 Complete each sentence with a word or phrase from the box. Sometimes more than one answer is possible.

| although | however | in spite of | on the other hand | nevertheless |

1. This is a great city; *nevertheless / however*, it's too crowded.
2. _____ living downtown is expensive, there's a lot to do.
3. The summer is beautiful here. _____, it's terrible in the winter.
4. _____ the high crime rate, I'm not afraid to walk home alone after dark.

4A Reduced time clauses

In a reduced time clause, the subject of the clause is omitted and the verb is changed to an *-ing* form. A time clause with *before*, *after*, or *while* can be reduced only if the subject in the sentence's other clause is the same.
Before **I go to sleep**, I like to read.
Before **going to sleep**, I like to read.
I like to read before **going to sleep**.
Before **the baby goes to sleep, his mother reads** to him.

Once, every time, till, as, the first / next / last time, and many other time expressions can be used in time clauses. Time clauses beginning with these expressions cannot be reduced.
As soon as / Once I drink that first cup of coffee, I'm ready for the day.
Whenever / Every time I stay out late, I have trouble getting up the next morning.
I always stay at the office **until / till** I've finished all my work.
I like to watch TV **as** I'm eating dinner.
The last time I drank too much coffee, I was jittery all day.

1 Which of these time clauses can be reduced (*R*)? Which ones cannot be reduced (*N*)? Write the correct letter.

  _N_ 1. Ever since I can remember, I've been a night owl.
  ____ 2. Once I fall asleep, I almost never wake up until morning.
  ____ 3. My mother races off to work right after I leave for school.
  ____ 4. Every time Jerry comes to visit, he keeps me up past my bedtime.
  ____ 5. As soon as I get up in the morning, I drink a large glass of water.
  ____ 6. I always listen to music while I run.
  ____ 7. I often doze off as I'm watching TV at night.
  ____ 8. Whenever I drink coffee after 3:00, I have trouble falling asleep.
  ____ 9. I always have breakfast at a local café before I start classes for the day.
  ____ 10. The last time I stayed at a hotel, the bed was really uncomfortable.

2 Rewrite the sentences using reduced time clauses.

1. I usually watch the news while I have breakfast.
   I usually watch the news while having breakfast.

2. My sister won't drink orange juice after she brushes her teeth.

3. She does a lot of housework before she leaves for work in the morning.

4. Power nappers work better after they sleep for a short time during the day.

5. You probably shouldn't eat anything heavy before you exercise.

6. If I listen to soft music while I study, I can concentrate better.

7. After I'm in an argument, I need to be by myself for an hour or two.

8. Before I chill out at night, I make sure everything is ready for the morning.

4B Clauses stating reasons and conditions

The following are all additional commonly used clauses that state reasons and conditions.

Now that introduces a change in general circumstances that explains the main clause. ***Now that*** means "because now."
Now that I have a job that starts early, I have to leave the house by 6:30.

Whether or not introduces a condition that might or might not occur and which will not influence the main clause. Note its two possible positions.
She goes jogging every morning **whether or not** it's bad weather.
She goes jogging every morning **whether** it's bad weather **or not**.

Provided / Providing (***that***) introduces a condition that must be met for the main clause to be true.
Provided that I get all my schoolwork done, my weekend will be free.
Providing that I get a promotion, I'll stay with my company a few more years.

1 Match each sentence on the left with the best meaning on the right.

1. She always has breakfast whether she's in a hurry or not. _c_
2. Now that she works the afternoon shift, she always has time for breakfast. ____
3. Unless her mother makes it, she doesn't bother with breakfast. ____
4. She only eats breakfast if she's hungry. ____
5. Provided that she has enough time, she has breakfast. ____
6. As long as she has breakfast, she can concentrate in class. ____

a. She has plenty of time to eat something in the morning.
b. She skips her morning meal when she doesn't feel like eating anything.
c. She eats something every morning.
d. When she is in a hurry, she doesn't eat breakfast.
e. She never makes her own morning meal.
f. If she doesn't eat, she can't think clearly.

2 Choose the correct answer to complete the sentence.

1. He won't be late for work *as long as* / *unless* the bus is on time.
2. *Considering that* / *Just in case* I took a nap, I shouldn't feel this drowsy.
3. I'll wake up on time tomorrow, *provided that* / *unless* I set my alarm clock.
4. He jogs after work *now that* / *unless* he's too tired at the end of the day.
5. My brother usually goes to bed early *now that* / *whether or not* he's sleepy.
6. *Now that* / *Even if* I'm going to bed later, I'm getting up later.
7. I'm afraid to nap at lunch *even if* / *just in case* I start snoring at my desk.
8. *Even if* / *Provided that* I'm totally exhausted, I can't sleep on airplanes.

5A Infinitive and gerund phrases

> In a sentence with *It's* + adjective + infinitive, it is possible to follow the adjective with *for* and an object. The object can be a pronoun or a noun.
> **It's difficult for her to talk** about her feelings openly.
> **It's customary for North Americans to make** frequent eye contact.
>
> For sentences in the negative, use *not* + infinitive or *not* + gerund.
> It's considered rude **not to thank** people who give you gifts.
> **Not thanking** people who give you gifts is considered rude.
>
> Adjectives of feeling (*glad*, *happy*, *pleased*) cannot be used with the *It's* + adjective + infinitive structure. Instead, the sentence needs to say who has (or doesn't have) these feelings.
> **Most parents are happy to see** their children go to college.
> **People are always delighted to get** compliments.

1 Rewrite the sentences using infinitive or gerund phrases.

1. It's important to make a good first impression.
   Making a good first impression is important.
2. Arriving late for an appointment is inappropriate in most countries.
3. It's fairly typical for college students to get to a party late.
4. It's considered rude not to be punctual for a dinner party.
5. Keeping the conversation going is easy for Elyse.
6. Showing the bottom of your feet is offensive in some places.
7. It's good form to bring a small gift to a dinner party.
8. Talking about politics is sometimes risky.
9. It's customary for some parents to brag about their children.
10. Thanking the hostess the day after a party is a nice idea.

2 Write sentences with infinitive phrases using the words below.

1. Tom / always happy / lend money to his friends
   Tom is always happy to lend money to his friends.
2. Wendy / unusual / arrive late to class
   It's unusual for Wendy to arrive late to class.
3. Donald / relaxing / not have homework over the weekend
4. Min / always glad / help a friend in need
5. many tourists / surprised / learn about some American customs
6. students / inappropriate / interrupt a teacher
7. new employees / often afraid / ask their bosses for help
8. dinner guests / customary / thank their hosts
9. businesspeople / important / be punctual for appointments

5B Reported speech

The modals *can*, *may*, *must*, *have to*, and *don't have to* change in reported speech. *Might* and *should* do not change. Also notice how the pronouns change in reported speech.

Statements
"You **can** go to the party with **me**."
"I **may** go to a movie tonight."
"We **must** tell him the truth."
"He **has to** go to the bank."
"You **don't have to** pay **me** back."
"We **might** get married."
"I **should** replace **my** old laptop."

Reported statements
She said I **could** go to the party with **her**.
He said he **might** go to a movie tonight.
They said they **had to** tell him the truth.
He said he **had to** go to the bank.
She said I **didn't have to** pay **her** back.
She said they **might** get married.
He said he **should** replace **his** old laptop.

Say and *tell* are used differently in reported speech. *Tell* must be followed by a noun or object pronoun. *Say* is not followed by a noun/pronoun object.

Statements
"Don't park the car there."

Reported statements
She **told me** not to park the car there.
She **said** not to park the car there.

When a very recent statement is being reported, no tense change is necessary.
A: I didn't hear that. What did she say?
B: She said she **wants** to go out for dinner.

Review the rules for reported speech on page 41. Change these conversations to reported speech.

1. Ryan: I'm thinking of applying for a promotion at work.
   Emma: What kind of promotion is it?
   Ryan: Our department needs a new manager.
   Emma: You should definitely apply!
   Ryan: I'm a little nervous because there's a big interview.
   Emma: You just have to practice. I can help you.
   Ryan told Emma he was thinking of applying for a promotion at work.

2. Karl: Do we have to sign up for our after-school club?
   Tanya: You can sign up until noon.
   Ava: Don't wait too long. The good clubs are filling up fast.
   Karl: I'll do it after I eat my lunch.

3. Larry: I'm going to the Galápagos Islands in April.
   Jason: That's wonderful! You must send me some photos.
   Larry: I'll send you some. I promise! But why don't you go with me?
   Jason: I can't go. I may be starting a new job in April.

6A Present perfect vs. simple past

> Use the present perfect to report a repeated past event that could continue into the present.
> Thieves **have robbed** three banks this year.
> The seal **has painted** four pictures so far.

> Use the present perfect to report an event that has an effect on the present, or is still relevant.
> She**'s been** more careful since she lost her car keys.
> The store **has had** a security camera for a month now.

1 Complete these sentences with the simple past or the present perfect form of the verbs in parentheses.

1. The police ____caught____ (catch) the robber when he _____ (sell) the stolen art.
2. Unbelievably, the same woman _____ (win) the lottery twice since May.
3. So far, the children _____ (raise) more than $500 for charity.
4. Since the city _____ (pass) its new laws last year, crime _____ (fall).
5. The kidnappers _____ (not call) and _____ (not demand) any ransom yet.
6. No storms _____ (strike) since the summer _____ (begin).

6A Present perfect vs. present perfect continuous

> Some verbs, such as *live, work, study, give/take (lessons),* and *teach,* express the idea of an ongoing action. They can usually be used in either the present perfect or the present perfect continuous.
> He **has lived** in London for eight years.
> I **have taken** violin lessons since I was three.
> He **has been living** in London for eight years.
> I **have been taking** violin lessons since I was three.

2 Review the rules for the present perfect and the present perfect continuous on page 45. Then choose the correct form of the verb to complete the article. Sometimes more than one answer is possible.

It's a sad day for many who (1) *have lived* / *have been living* in this town since they were children. The town council (2) *has decided* / *has been deciding* to take down the old fishing pier.

Fisherman Bob Kates said, "I (3) *have worked* / *have been working* here since I was young. Generations of kids (4) *have taken* / *have been taking* swimming lessons here. I myself (5) *have jumped* / *have been jumping* off this pier many times, especially on hot summer days. However, today the temperature (6) *has reached* / *has been reaching* 36 degrees Celsius, but nobody can jump off the pier as the town (7) *has already put up* / *has already been putting up* barriers. It's true that the pier (8) *has been* / *has been being* in pretty bad condition for a while now, so I guess it's a safety issue."

It's not all bad news for Mr. Kates. The town (9) *has studied* / *has been studying* proposals for replacing the pier for a year now, and in fact, planning for a new and improved pier (10) *has already begun* / *has already been beginning*.

6B Adverbs with the simple past and past perfect

When and the simple past and past perfect can be used to express different time relationships.
When I arrived in Bangkok, my connecting flight **had already departed**.
When I arrived in Bangkok, my friend **met** me at the airport.

When *before* makes the sequence of events clear, the simple past or past perfect can be used.
It **began** to rain **before** she boarded the plane.
It **had begun** to rain **before** she boarded the plane.

Yet and *already* are used with both the present perfect and past perfect to show that an event took place earlier.
It **had already started** raining when I arrived in Bangkok.
It **hadn't started** raining **yet** when I arrived in Bangkok.

Choose the correct form of the verb to complete the story.

The taxi arrived to take Erica to the airport for her flight to London. Until that day she (1) *was never /* (had never been) on an international flight. The travel agent (2) *told / had told* her to get to the airport early, so she (3) *arrived / had arrived* four hours before her flight was due to leave. When she (4) *got / had gotten* there, she (5) *realized / had realized* she had plenty of time to spare, so she (6) *decided / had decided* to have some coffee and a snack and look at the newspaper before she (7) *checked in / had checked in*. She (8) *already bought / had already bought* some chocolate bars to eat on the plane, so she decided to have one of those. She sat at the counter and ordered a coffee.

When her coffee (9) *came / had come*, she pulled her favorite section out of the newspaper, carefully refolded it, and put it on the counter beside her. When she (10) *reached / had reached* for her chocolate bar, she saw that someone (11) *already took / had already taken* it out of the package and (12) *broke / had broken* it into eight tidy squares. She looked beside her and saw a distinguished-looking businessman. Before that, she (13) *didn't really notice / hadn't really noticed* him. She watched as he picked up a piece of the chocolate and calmly popped it into his mouth. She (14) *never saw / had never seen* such rude behavior in her life, so still staring at him, she (15) *picked up / had picked up* a piece and ate it. By now, he was staring back. He picked up another piece and ate it. So did Erica. Finally, there was only one piece left. Erica (16) *took / had taken* it.

The man stood up. He said, "Look. If you're that hungry, buy yourself a donut!" He (17) *slammed / had slammed* a dollar bill down on the counter and stormed out. In her entire life, she (18) *was never / had never been* so shocked. Muttering to herself, Erica began to gather up her things. Suddenly, she stopped, standing as still as a statue. There, under her newspaper, (19) *was / had been* her chocolate bar, exactly where she (20) *put / had put* it before the whole fiasco began.

7A Passive of present continuous, present perfect, future

> If the agent (the person or thing doing the action) is unknown or obvious from the context, it's better to use a passive form. However, if the person or thing doing the action needs to be emphasized, it's better to use an active form.
> The spyware **is being used** to collect information about college students. *(Agent is unknown.)*
> Social networking sites **have been used** in criminal investigations. *(Agent is clear from context.)*
> A criminal organization **has created** this virus, not an amateur hacker. *(Agent is emphasized.)*
>
> **The passive is very rarely used with the present perfect continuous. Use the passive of the present perfect instead.**
> People **have been posting** more videos to the Internet this year than ever before.
> More videos **have been posted** to the Internet this year than ever before.

1 For each pair of sentences, is it better to use the passive or active form? Choose *a* or *b*.

1. ☑ a. More U.S. employers will likely allow access to social networking sites.
   ☐ b. Access to social networking sites will likely be allowed.

2. ☐ a. Soon, inventors will invent smartphones that don't require a battery.
   ☐ b. Smartphones that don't require a battery will be invented soon.

3. ☐ a. Most cell phone companies are now offering unlimited-use plans.
   ☐ b. Unlimited-use plans are being offered now.

4. ☐ a. Teachers might be teaching more high school students with educational computer games.
   ☐ b. More high school students might be taught with educational computer games.

2 Complete the sentences with the correct active or passive form of the verb in parentheses.

1. Recently, social networking sites _have become_ (become) popular with all age groups.

2. Every week, free software _____ (download) on computers everywhere.

3. In the years to come, podcasts _____ (use) more often in educational programs.

4. Lately, children _____ (ask) for cell phones at a younger and younger age.

5. More sophisticated viruses _____ (create) all the time.

6. For years, hackers _____ (try) to use spyware to commit identity theft.

7. In years to come, more and more data _____ (store) in the cloud.

8. I recently discovered that my neighbors _____ (use) my Wi-Fi many times.

9. In the next decade, more job interviews _____ (hold) online.

10. Since I last visited this blog, several older posts _____ (remove).

7B Negative and tag questions for giving opinions

> Use past negative and tag questions to offer an opinion about a past event and invite someone to react.
> **Wasn't it** weird how the manager's microphone kept turning on and off during his speech?
> **Didn't it seem** like the manager's speech would never end?
> **Shouldn't the company have provided** us with coffee before the speech?
> The manager's speech was really boring, **wasn't it**?
> The manager has given some pretty boring speeches, **hasn't he**?
> The manager's speech had just put about everyone to sleep when the fire alarm rang, **hadn't it**?
>
> In informal spoken English, *they* can be used as the pronoun in tag questions when the subject is *somebody, someone, everybody, everyone, nobody,* or *no one.*
> **Everyone** we know had a cell phone in school, didn't **they**? Yes, they did.
> **Somebody** has hacked into your computer, haven't **they**? Yes, they have. / No, they haven't.
>
> Use an affirmative tag question when the subject is a negative, such as *nobody* or *nothing*.
> **Nobody** left any voice mail messages, **did they**? Yes, they did. / No, they didn't.

1 Turn the statements into negative questions.

1. It would have been great if telemarketers had never gotten my number.
   Wouldn't it have been great if telemarketers had never gotten my number?
2. It was awful how much paper we wasted on fliers that nobody read.
3. Jill should have kept her text messages much shorter.
4. It was weird how those pop-up ads made my computer freeze.
5. It seemed like we spent all day looking for an Internet café.
6. It would have been great if we could have paid less for our computer.
7. We should have spent less time playing video games as kids.
8. It was sad how Mark got really addicted to social networking sites.

2 Complete the sentences with tag questions.

1. There were several voice mail messages for me, *weren't there*?
2. There haven't been any new rules about using social media at work, _____?
3. Someone told him there was a problem with his phone, _____?
4. You gave your computer password to someone, _____?
5. There was nothing he could do with his obsolete computer, _____?
6. Nobody we know ever actually clicked on those banner ads, _____?
7. She had already complained about the telemarketers, _____?
8. You used to have a robot vacuum that constantly cleaned the house, _____?

8A Reduced relative clauses

> **Non-defining relative clauses with *be* can be reduced in the same way as defining relative clauses. Notice the use of commas.**
> Einstein**, who is thought to be one of the greatest minds of the twentieth century,** struggled in school.
> Einstein**, thought to be one of the greatest minds of the twentieth century,** struggled in school.
> Curtis James Jackson III**, who is better known as the singer 50 Cent,** used to be a boxer.
> Curtis James Jackson III**, better known as the singer 50 Cent,** used to be a boxer.

1 Rewrite these sentences using reduced relative clauses.

1. The photographer who lives upstairs has won many awards for his creativity.
   The photographer living upstairs has won many awards for his creativity.

2. Professional cooking, which is considered a tough business, requires both patience and skill.

3. Movie stars who are constantly hounded by the press deserve more privacy.

4. Roger Federer, who is ranked among the world's best tennis players, is considered very disciplined.

5. The Summer Olympics, which are held every four years, are broadcast around the world.

6. Children who are talented at music should take private lessons if possible.

2 Combine the sentences. Rewrite them as one sentence containing a reduced non-defining relative clause.

1. Lady Gaga is generally believed to be very confident and professional. She claims she is actually shy.
   Lady Gaga, generally believed to be very confident and professional, claims she is actually shy.

2. Yohji Yamamoto is famous for his modern fashion designs. He often uses the color black.

3. Jessica Alba has been interested in acting since the age of five. She first appeared in a film at age 13.

4. The movie *Twilight* was adapted from a novel by Stephenie Meyer. It stars Robert Pattinson.

5. Mark Zuckerberg is celebrated for creating Facebook. He attended Harvard University.

6. Justin Bieber is originally from Canada. He began his professional singing career in the U.S.

7. Tim Berners-Lee is credited with inventing the Web. He published the first website in 1991.

8. Jamie Oliver is known for his food-focused TV shows. He advocates healthier food in schools.

8B Non-defining relative clauses as sentence modifiers

Non-defining relative clauses can be used as sentence modifiers and can contain almost any verb. Some of the most common ones are *surprise*, *depress*, *encourage*, *suggest (that)*, *contribute to*, and *result in*. Note that the verbs that describe emotion must be followed by an object.

My husband tried to repair a leak with aluminum foil, **which has resulted in a ruined silk carpet**.
My teacher praised my English today, **which encourages me to study harder**.
Peter has been happier since he took up golf, **which suggests that hobbies are good for a person both mentally and physically**.
I learned how to clean jewelry with toothpaste, **which depressed me because it meant I had wasted a fortune on expensive cleaners**.
I've started making my own clothes, **which has contributed to financial savings and a full closet**!

1 Match these statements with the appropriate non-defining clauses.

1. I use dental floss to string beads for jewelry, __c__
2. My sister always loved school, ____
3. Robert moved to a small town, ____
4. I just had a big fight with Ana, ____
5. Paul is really good at solving problems, ____
6. Amy jogs every morning, ____
7. I've had a private tutor for the past few months, ____
8. The class I wanted to take is already full, ____

a. which surprised us since he loves cities.
b. which has contributed to weight loss and more energy.
c. which is why I have so much of it.
d. which is why people always go to him for help.
e. which has resulted in better grades for me.
f. which encouraged her to go into teaching.
g. which means I'll have to explore alternatives in the course schedule.
h. which depressed me because she's my best friend.

2 Complete the sentences with a phrase from the box.

| which resulted in | which suggested | which depressed |
| which encouraged | which means | which surprised |

1. I'm working late tonight, _____which means_____ I'll take a later train home.
2. My friend was in a local play, _____ me to try acting.
3. Our team lost the championship, _____ me and my friends.
4. Prices went down last year, _____ savings for many people.
5. Ted sent me a nice birthday card, _____ me since he usually doesn't do anything special for people's birthdays.
6. Dinner tasted terrible, _____ that I didn't follow the recipe correctly.

9A Clauses and phrases showing contrast and exception

> The following are additional common phrases that show contrast and exception.
>
> Use **whereas**, especially in formal writing, to present contrasting information.
> **Whereas** the bottled water market is huge in Italy, it is very small in Japan.
>
> Use **except (for)** or **with the exception of** to show an exception within a group.
> Everyone in my family, **except for** my mother, plays a musical instrument.
> Everyone in my family, **with the exception of** my mother, plays a musical instrument.

1 Circle the correct answer to complete the sentence.

1. (While) / *Unlike* Leo prefers a big breakfast, I just have coffee.
2. No one in the class, *except that / with the exception of* Eva, can speak German.
3. *In contrast to / While* city people, those who live on farms must have a car.
4. *Unlike / Except for* Thai women, Spanish women greet each other with a kiss.
5. I'm a typical Canadian, *whereas / except for the fact that* I don't like hockey.
6. Most Americans have dinner by 7:00, *whereas / unlike* in Spain people eat later.
7. Everyone on our street, *except that / except for* my family, has a pet.
8. *Unlike / While* me, all my friends are addicted to reality shows on TV.

2 Read about Alonzo and Jun. Complete the sentences with an expression to show contrast or exception. More than one answer is possible.

Alonzo (26 years old) . . .	Jun (21 years old) . . .
finished college four years ago.	is in his third year of college.
considers himself to be pretty typical.	doesn't think he's really typical.
plays and watches all kinds of sports.	doesn't play any sports.
isn't crazy about baseball.	doesn't watch any sport but baseball.
has a high salary and eats out often.	doesn't work and always cooks at home.
wears a suit on weekdays.	always dresses very casually.

1. Jun is still in college, *whereas / while* Alonzo has already graduated.
2. Alonzo considers himself to be pretty typical, _____ Jun doesn't.
3. _____ Jun, Alonzo is a big sports fan.
4. Alonzo is a fan of most sports _____ baseball.
5. Alonzo has dinner in restaurants, _____ Jun usually can't afford to eat out.
6. _____ Alonzo, Jun hardly ever dresses up.
7. Alonzo has a good job, _____ Jun isn't working now.
8. Jun and Alonzo are very different, _____ they are both in their 20s.

9B Past habitual with *used to* and *would*

> To ask questions about a habitual action or situation in the past, use *Did . . . use to . . . ?* (NOT *Would . . . ?*).
> **Did you use to listen** to rock music when you were younger?
> **Did you use to share** a bedroom with your little brother?
>
> Use the negative question *Didn't . . . use to . . . ?* to confirm a guess about habitual actions or a situation in the past.
> **Didn't you use to work** at a grocery store after school?
> **Didn't he use to play** on the school soccer team?

1 Write the questions to these responses. Use *Did . . . use to* or *Didn't . . . use to*.

1. A: <u>Did / Didn't you use to live in San Francisco?</u>
   B: Yes, I did. I lived in San Francisco for about two years.

2. A: _____
   B: A lot? No, as a matter of fact, I've never drunk coffee.

3. A: _____
   B: No, he never did. Actually, Pete's allergic to cats.

4. A: _____
   B: In the school band? Yes, I did. I played the flute.

5. A: _____
   B: Yes, I always rode my bike in elementary school, but I'd take the bus on rainy days.

6. A: _____
   B: Yeah, my hair was really long, but I had to cut it when I joined the swim team.

2 Choose the correct answer to complete each sentence. Sometimes both are possible.

1. Lesley *would* / *(used to)* live in Brazil before she moved to Turkey.
2. We *would* / *used to* have fun during summer vacations.
3. They *would* / *used to* have a house by the ocean, but they've sold it.
4. Serena *would* / *used to* go mountain biking every weekend.
5. *Would her parents* / *Did her parents use to* own a Mexican restaurant ten years ago?
6. My mother *would* / *used to* volunteer at the hospital every winter.
7. Alex *would* / *used to* like to build models of cars and ships.
8. *Would you* / *Did you use to* be good at fixing cars when you were younger?

10A Relative clauses and noun clauses

> In some relative clauses, the relative pronoun (*who*, *that*, or *which*) can be omitted.
>
> **In an object relative clause, a relative pronoun (*who*, *that*, or *which*) is optional. Relative pronouns are only required when they function as the subject of a relative clause.**
> My friend told our classmates a secret. I had told him that secret.
> My friend told our classmates a secret (**that**) I had told him.
>
> **In a subject relative clause, a relative pronoun (*who*, *that*, or *which*) is necessary because it functions as the subject of the relative clause.**
> I have a roommate. She never cleans the kitchen.
> I have a roommate **who** never cleans the kitchen.

1 Choose the sentences where the relative pronoun (*who*, *that*, or *which*) is optional.

- ☑ 1. The restaurant that we had dinner at last night overcharged us.
- ☐ 2. One thing that makes me sick is really selfish people.
- ☐ 3. People who chew gum loudly really get on my nerves.
- ☐ 4. Someone's cell phone kept ringing all through the movie that I saw last night.
- ☐ 5. I had a big argument with a store clerk who refused to give me a refund.
- ☐ 6. My teacher gets mad at every little noise that our class makes.
- ☐ 7. The town fined a neighbor who burned garbage in her backyard.
- ☐ 8. The people in the line which he tried to cut into complained to the theater manager.

2 Complete the sentences with *who* or *that*. If the pronoun can be omitted, write *X*. Sometimes more than one answer is possible.

1. One thing ____that____ gets me down is people __who / that__ lie to me.
2. I like people _____ stand up for something _____ they believe in.
3. Something _____ makes me sad is people _____ have no place to live.
4. Something _____ I can't do is keep up with technology.
5. I was a kid _____ had parents _____ made a lot of rules.
6. The thing _____ aggravates me most is people _____ are cruel to animals.

10B Simple and complex indirect questions

> If the beginning clause of an indirect question is in statement word order, the sentence is a statement and ends with a period.
> **I'm curious about** why he didn't complain to the landlord.
> **I'm not sure** who is responsible for repairing the roads.
> **The big question is** if / whether we can get the city officials to listen to our concerns.
>
> If the beginning clause of an indirect question is in question word order, the sentence is a question and ends with a question mark.
> **Do you have any idea** if / whether I need a visa to visit China?
> **Could you tell me** where I can go to pay my parking ticket?
> **Don't you wonder** how a place with such poor service stays in business?

1 Rewrite these sentences using the words in parentheses.

1. Why can't the city add more streetlights? (I don't understand . . .)
   I don't understand why the city can't add more streetlights.

2. Is the city going to improve the rush hour bus service? (Do you know . . .)

3. Why are prices going up so fast? (. . . is something that baffles me.)

4. How can I finish the work before the deadline? (I have no idea . . .)

5. Have you saved enough money for school? (Would you mind telling me . . .)

6. Why aren't there any bike paths in the city? (. . . is beyond me.)

7. How am I going to find time to enjoy myself? (My main problem is . . .)

8. When are they going to build a new hospital? (Do you have any idea . . .)

9. Who decided to close the swimming pool in the park? (Don't you wonder . . .)

10. Is tuition going up again next year? (I have to find out . . .)

2 Rewrite these sentences as direct questions.

1. I haven't got a clue what we're supposed to do for homework tonight.
   What are we supposed to do for homework tonight?

2. How people can leave their children home alone is mystifying to me.

3. What I don't get is how I can keep up with all this new technology.

4. Why there isn't a pedestrian zone downtown is my number-one question.

5. I'd like to know who should be responsible for keeping our city clean.

6. Tell me what I have to do to get my driver's license.

7. When the next meeting will be is something I haven't found out yet.

8. I wonder if I should complain about my neighbor's loud parties.

11A Present unreal conditional with *unless*, *only if*, and *even if*

> To ask a follow-up question after a yes/no question, a shortened conditional can be used, especially in spoken or informal English. The positive shortened conditional is *if so*, and the negative shortened conditional is *if not*.
> Would you consider lying to a good friend to avoid hurting your friend's feelings? **If so**, what kinds of things would you lie about?
> Are you sure your friends are loyal and trusting? **If not**, you shouldn't tell them your secrets.

1 Match the yes/no questions on the left with the follow-up questions on the right.

1. Would you say anything if a colleague called you by the wrong name? _c_
2. If the man next to you on the bus fell asleep on your shoulder, would you wake him up? ____
3. Would you remain silent if you disagreed with your boss in a meeting? ____
4. Would you report it if you saw a friend steal a small item from a store? ____
5. If people you secretly disliked invited you to a party at their home, would you go? ____
6. If a cat always came to your house for food, would you keep it? ____

a. If not, what would you say?
b. If not, would you confront your friend?
c. If so, what would you say?
d. If not, would you try to find its owner?
e. If so, how would you wake him up?
f. If not, what excuse would you give?

2 Review the rules for the present unreal conditional with *unless*, *only if*, and *even if* on page 89. Choose the correct answer to complete each sentence.

1. I wouldn't lie to a friend (*unless*) / *only if* it was in his or her best interests.
2. If you found money on the street, would you turn it in to the police?
   If so / *If not*, what would you do with it?
3. Would you report a shoplifter *only if* / *even if* the person looked poor?
   If so / *If not*, would you tell the store manager, or would you call the police?
4. He wouldn't lose his temper *only if* / *even if* he were really angry.
5. Would you confront a friend who gossiped about you behind your back?
   If so / *If not*, what would you say?
6. I wouldn't read anyone else's mail *even if* / *only if* I were really curious.
7. Would you make a promise if you already knew you couldn't keep it?
   If so / *If not*, what would you do later when you didn't keep the promise?
8. I would criticize my friends *unless* / *only if* I knew a way to help them improve.

11B Wishes and regrets

Wishes and regrets often use comparative words, such as *(not) enough*, *more*, *less*, and *better*, and intensifiers, such as *really* and *very*.

I did**n't** save **enough** money last summer.
I wish I had saved **more** money last summer.

I spent **too much** money on video games last year.
If only I had spent **less** money on video games last year.

I bought **too many** clothes this weekend.
I wish I had bought **fewer** clothes this weekend.

I do**n't** understand math very **well**.
I wish I understood math **better**.

I got **really** angry at my friend last night.
If only I had**n't** gotten **so** angry at my friend last night.

1 Complete the wishes and regrets with a word from the box.

| better | fewer | harder | less | more | so |

1. I don't have enough time to do volunteer work.
   I wish I had ____*more*____ time to do volunteer work.

2. I don't know how to swim very well.
   I wish I knew how to swim _____.

3. I drank too much coffee before bed last night.
   If only I had drunk _____ coffee before bed last night.

4. The teacher thought the questions on the exam were much too easy.
   The teacher wished the questions on the exam had been _____.

5. Our class has too many assignments this week.
   I wish our class had _____ assignments this week.

6. I felt really sleepy in class and couldn't pay any attention.
   I wish I hadn't felt _____ sleepy in class and had paid attention.

2 Rewrite these sentences using the words in parentheses.

1. I wasn't very obedient in elementary school. (I wish . . .)
   I wish I had been more obedient in elementary school.

2. I refused to take piano lessons when I was young. (If only . . .)

3. I fell asleep at the computer last night, and now my essay is late. (I wish . . . Then . . .)

4. I exercised too much yesterday, so now I feel really tired. (If only . . . Then . . .)

5. Bob is shy and doesn't make friends easily. (Bob wishes . . .)

6. I'm not a very good cook. (If only . . .)

12A Future perfect and future perfect continuous

> When using the future perfect or future perfect continuous, the particular point in the future is often referred to in another part of the sentence.
> **By this time next year**, your commitment to language study is going to have gotten stronger.
> **On August 1**, I will have been living overseas for six months.
> **After a few months**, you're going to have made real progress with English.
> **Before next spring**, he will have finished most of his course work.
> **By the time you arrive in New York**, Marisa will have already received the package you sent.
> **When the van arrives**, I will have been packing for two days, and I probably won't have finished.
> **Before I leave for Paris**, I will already have sold my house and put my things in storage.
> **After I finish this**, I will have completed everything on my "to do" list.

1 Underline the words in each sentence that refer to a point in the future.

1. <u>By the spring</u>, Nate will have visited over a dozen different countries.
2. When the end of the week arrives, I will have written four exams.
3. Before long, I'll have been working on this puzzle for an hour. It's impossible!
4. I can't believe he's still sleeping! At 11:00, he'll have been sleeping for 12 hours.
5. When she leaves the house, she'll have had six cups of coffee.
6. If it continues, on Tuesday it will have been raining for three weeks.
7. After I stop working, I will have painted three of the rooms in my house.
8. By the time the plane lands, we will have been in the air for seven hours.

2 Complete the sentences with the future perfect or the future perfect continuous form of the verb in parentheses.

1. By the end of class, I ___*will have learned*___ (learn) about the future perfect tense.
2. By the year 2030, I _____ (work) for several years.
3. Before she's 30, Sue _____ (make) her first million dollars.
4. At the end of his trip, Seth _____ (visit) four different countries.
5. After I finish this book, I _____ (read) all the titles you recommended.
6. By 11:00, how long _____ Dan _____ (watch) TV?
7. When I finish college, I _____ (be) in school for 16 years.
8. Pretty soon, I _____ (wait) for her for an hour. I'm getting annoyed!
9. We're late. By the time we get there, they _____ (finish) dinner.
10. On Friday of this week, Kara _____ (travel) for two months.

12B Mixed conditionals

Conditionals can appear in many forms. They can describe how situations in the past affect situations in the past, the present, or the future.

Use a past form in both the *if* clause and the result clause to talk about true events in the past.
When I was younger, if I **didn't behave** well, my parents **were** disappointed.
If we **got** lost during our trip last year, we just **asked** someone for directions.

Use the past perfect in the *if* clause and *would / wouldn't have* + the past participle of the verb in the result clause to talk about hypothetical situations in the past that had effects on the more recent past.
If I **had been born** with a good voice, I **would have started** my own band a long time ago.

Use the past perfect in the *if* clause and *would / wouldn't* + verb in the result clause to describe hypothetical situations in the past that have effects on the present.
If I **had studied** harder when I was in school, I **would have** a better job today.

Use the past perfect in the *if* clause and *would / wouldn't* + verb in the result clause to talk about hypothetical situations in the past that have effects on the future.
If she **had booked** her flight before now, she **would be** in Paris next week.
If I **hadn't taken** a year off from school, I **would be graduating** this June.

Complete these sentences with the correct form of the verbs in parentheses. Sometimes more than one answer is possible.

1. As a kid, I always ___enjoyed___ (enjoy) school if I _____ (like) the teacher.
2. If I _____ (study) harder last year, I _____ (not have to) repeat the course this year.
3. If he _____ (not speak) Greek, his trip to Athens last year _____ (be) so enjoyable.
4. When I was young, if I _____ (see) a scary movie, I _____ (have) bad dreams.
5. When I was a kid, if my father _____ (go away) on a business trip, he always _____ (call) at 8:00 to say "Good night" to us.
6. If I _____ (spend) less money when I was younger, I _____ (have) a nice little nest egg in a few years.
7. If I _____ (not have) a fight with my friend yesterday, I _____ (go) to the party tonight.
8. If she _____ (show) more interest since she was hired, she _____ (get) the next promotion.
9. If I _____ (not lose) my passport, I _____ (fly) to Lisbon tonight.
10. If she _____ (not start) figure skating when she was four, she _____ (not be) in the last Olympics.

VOCABULARY PLUS

1A Personality collocations

Choose the correct words to complete the sentences.

1. I'm thinking about different careers. Since most people think I'm *calm and cool* / *wild and crazy* / *friendly and outgoing*, I'd probably be a good air traffic controller. Also, I love planes! **–Jen**

2. I enjoy shopping and have always wanted to work in retail. My family thinks I'm *friendly and outgoing* / *shy and reserved* / *neat and tidy* and advises me to become a sales manager. **–Eva**

3. I'll do anything to make people laugh. My friends think I'm *wild and crazy* / *laid-back and relaxed* / *kind and generous*. They think I might have a future as a comedian. **–Matt**

4. I've traveled to many countries on my own. Since I'm *laid-back and relaxed* / *neat and tidy* / *strong and independent* and enjoy photography, I want to become a photojournalist. It would be exciting to travel around the world to cover major news events. **–Paolo**

5. I tend to be *friendly and outgoing* / *shy and reserved* / *honest and sincere*, so I prefer to work alone. I plan to become a software developer. **–Jim**

1B Compound family terms

Combine the prefixes and the suffix with some of the words for family members to complete the conversation. Some prefixes will be used more than once.

| great- | grand- | great-grand- | -in-law |

| aunt | brother | father | mother | nephew | niece | uncle |

Sara: Hi, Alex! The whole family is here at the wedding! Do you see my (1) _great-grandmother_ over there?

Alex: Is she your mom's grandmother or your dad's grandmother?

Sara: My mom's. And look, there's Raul. He's married to Hugo's older sister. He's Hugo's (2) _____, but they get along better than most brothers.

Alex: Who's your favorite relative?

Sara: Oh, my (3) _____ Vera, my grandmother's sister. Although Vera has five (4) _____ besides me, I'm probably the closest. She lived next door when I was growing up and taught me to play the guitar.

Alex: That's cool . . .

Sara: Hey, do you see my (5) _____ Pat making my dad laugh? Pat is my father's uncle. It's always fun to hear his stories!

Alex: So, who is the other person with them?

Sara: Oh, that's my (6) _____, you know, my dad's grandfather. Let's go and say hello.

2A Collocations with *problem*

Choose the correct words to complete the sentences.

Problem-Solving Tips

1. The best way to *run into* / *deal with* a problem is to figure out what it is.
2. After you *identify* / *ignore* a problem, analyze it and think of possible solutions.
3. It's a mistake to believe that if you *ignore* / *cause* a problem long enough, it will go away.
4. Don't *aggravate* / *run into* problems by worrying too much about them and coming up with poor solutions.
5. Sometimes discussing a problem with others will help you *cause* / *solve* it.
6. Don't blame your problems on other people. It's best just to *deal with* / *avoid* problems as soon as possible.

2B Verbs of belief

Replace the underlined words with the correct form of the word or phrase from the box that means the same thing.

1. **be positive · doubt · suppose**

   The archaeologist dug up pieces of pottery in the castle ruins. After studying the pottery markings, he was sure that it was from the 16th century. ___was positive___

2. **assume · be certain · have a hunch**

   Based on clues at the crime scene, the detective suspected that the husband must have known something about his wife's disappearance. _____

3. **guess · know for a fact · suppose**

   The accountant carefully reviewed his client's records and was certain that all of his earnings and expenses were reported correctly. _____

4. **be sure · doubt · suspect**

   After examining the brushstrokes of the painting, the art expert figured that it must be a forgery. _____

5. **be certain · have a hunch · suppose**

   The lab technician studied the tooth under a microscope. She was sure it belonged to a humpback whale. _____

6. **be positive · doubt · guess**

   When the reporter investigated the story, he had a hunch that the politician was lying about the bank loan. _____

3A Features of cities

Use five more words or phrases from the box to complete the conversation.

| climate | crime rate | hotels | neighborhood | transportation system |
| cuisine | green spaces | job market | nightlife | |

Su-ho: Where do you want to live after you finish college?

Ines: Well, I have to support myself and pay my rent and other expenses. That means I'll need to live in a city with a strong (1) __job market__.

Su-ho: Yeah. And you enjoy the outdoors, so you probably want parks and other (2) _____.

Ines: Yes, you're right. I want places to run and bike. I love being in the sun, so a place with a good (3) _____ is also important.

Su-ho: That's true. You always complain about the cold winters here. Oh, and I know you also love trying new restaurants.

Ines: You know me so well! I'll definitely want to explore restaurants with many different kinds of (4) _____.

Su-ho: What else do you want a city to offer?

Ines: Well, I love going to jazz clubs and concerts, so a city with an active (5) _____ would be perfect. How about you? What's important to you?

Su-ho: I'd like to live in a friendly (6) _____ where I can meet people. That will make it easier to live in a new city.

3B Compound terms for towns

Cross out the phrases that do <u>not</u> fit the meaning of the sentences.

1. Thousands of visitors come to this *resort town* / ~~rural town~~ / *tourist town* each year to enjoy its beaches, hotels, and restaurants.

2. This *industrial town* / *coastal town* / *mountain town* does not have many factories or businesses, but it has amazing views and clean air.

3. This *mountain town* / *coastal town* / *port town* is located in a valley near a river, with convenient access for boats and ships.

4. This *suburban town* / *industrial town* / *rural town* has many gardens that are famous for gorgeous flowers and fruit trees.

5. Not many people live in this *resort town* / *mountain town* / *suburban town*, but many people vacation here because it offers activities such as skiing and hiking.

6. Most of the people in this *border town* / *college town* / *suburban town* are elderly, so there isn't much of a nightlife.

4A Phrasal verbs related to energy and sleep

Choose the correct words to complete the sentences.

1. I'm feeling tired, and I have to write a paper tonight. I think I'll take a quick walk in the fresh air to *burn out / sleep over / (perk up)*.

2. Lea taught four English classes today, and tonight, she had to run a faculty meeting. She really needs to *race off / chill out / burn out* for a while.

3. Ben will have to leave for the airport at 5:00 in the morning. He should probably *turn in / perk up / calm down* early tonight.

4. Dina lives in a town that's over an hour away from her office. When she has to work late, she often *races off / calms down / sleeps over* at a friend's place near the office.

5. Ellen invited us over for a dinner party last night. I had a great time, but I had to *race off / doze off / calm down* to catch the last train home.

6. I enjoy reading mystery novels on the bus, but if I'm tired, I sometimes *sleep over / burn out / doze off* after reading just a few pages.

4B Expressions related to sleep

Cross out the phrases that do <u>not</u> fit the meaning of the sentences.

Val: I'm exhausted this morning. I (1) *had a sleepless night / ~~slept like a log~~ / tossed and turned* last night. I even had some warm milk at 2:00 and still couldn't get to sleep.

Eva: Have you ever thought of going to bed earlier? If you put on some soft music and relaxed, you'd probably (2) *be wide awake / nod off / feel drowsy* in 10 or 15 minutes.

Val: Yes, I've tried that, but it doesn't help. Maybe I should cut back on coffee. The caffeine may be the reason why I'm (3) *fast asleep / wide awake / tossing and turning* in the middle of the night.

Eva: I take a hot bath every night and am usually (4) *sleeping like a log / sound asleep / taking a power nap* by 10:30. Speaking of sleep, I hope I can stay awake tonight. It's 8:00, and I still have a lot of homework to finish.

Val: How about taking a quick power nap before doing your homework? That way, you won't (5) *drift off / be wide awake / feel drowsy* at your desk this evening.

5A Terms to describe behavior

Choose the correct words to complete the conversation.

Liu: I'm going to an academic conference in Los Angeles next week. It'll be my first time in the U.S., and I want to behave in an (1) *(appropriate)* / *offensive* / *unusual* way. Can I address people by their first names?

Jing: When you first meet people in the U.S., it's (2) *polite* / *offensive* / *rude* to address them by using their title and last name. Once you start talking, if the other person uses your first name, then you can do that as well.

Liu: OK, I'll try to remember that. Something else I want to know – do people kiss on the cheek when they first meet? Or is it better to shake hands?

Jing: In a professional setting, it's (3) *rude* / *strange* / *normal* to shake hands. Americans don't usually kiss strangers on the cheek.

Liu: I'm also wondering how to start conversations with people I meet for the first time.

Jing: Well, I think it's (4) *inappropriate* / *typical* / *bad form* to start by mentioning something interesting that a speaker said in a recent session. You might also ask someone's opinion about a conference topic.

Liu: OK. Now, sometimes when I get excited about an idea, I interrupt the other person with a lot of questions. Is that all right?

Jing: That's OK with friends, but when you meet new people, it's considered (5) *polite* / *a compliment* / *bad form*. You should let the other person finish talking.

5B Expressions for reported speech

Use phrases from each box to complete the conversations.

1. | advised me to | claimed that | promised to | wanted to know |

   A: My sister borrowed my car. She ___claimed that___ her car was being repaired.
   B: She _____ if I knew a good mechanic. It sounded like a big repair job!

2. | claimed that | encouraged me to | explained that | wondered |

   A: My parents _____ take a trip to Brazil this summer.
   B: That's fantastic! I _____ where you were planning to travel this year.

3. | advised me to | claimed that | wanted to know | warned me not to |

   A: My dad doesn't like my boyfriend because he plays in a band. He _____ find someone who's more serious about a career.
   B: My father thinks the same way. He _____ date artists or writers!

4. | advised me to | encouraged me to | explained that | promised to |

   A: Ted was late again! He _____ he'd been studying and lost track of time.
   B: Knowing Ted, I'll bet he _____ never be late again!

6A News events

Use four more events from the box to complete the headlines for the news stories.

Epidemic	Hijacking	Natural Disasters	Recession
Famine	Kidnapping	Political Crisis	Robbery

1. _Natural Disasters_ **Affect Economy**
   Last month's earthquake and storms caused significant damage to roads, bridges, and homes. The cost of repairs is putting a huge strain on the national economy.

2. _____ **of a Plane in Miami**
   Two men got on a plane at Miami National airport, threatened the pilots, and ordered them to fly to an unknown destination.

3. **Economy Falls into** _____
   Economists report that the unemployment rate has risen and consumer spending is slowing because people are saving money instead of purchasing goods.

4. _____ **Averted**
   The mayor is now under investigation and agreed to step down to avoid a government scandal. A special election will be held next month to fill his position.

5. **Experts Offer Tips to Prevent** _____
   Each year, thousands of people go missing. To prevent being taken against your will, security experts suggest that you change the routes you drive or walk every day and let your family or close friends know where you are going.

6B Storytelling expressions

Use phrases from each box to complete the story.

And in the end,	The next thing we knew,
I'll never forget the time	The thing you have to know is

(1) _I'll never forget the time_ it snowed in July. I was on vacation in the mountains with some friends, staying in a resort hotel. We went hiking and swimming every day. The weather was perfect – sunny and warm. One day, the temperature suddenly dropped, and the wind picked up. (2) _____ it was snowing big, fat flakes. It snowed for hours! (3) _____ that we were absolutely not ready for snow! We were wearing T-shirts, cotton pants, and sandals. Who knew we'd need snow boots in July?

It all started when	So finally,
I forgot to mention that	That reminds me of the time when

During the storm, we stayed inside, ordered sandwiches, and played board games. Oh, (4) _____ we lost electricity for a few hours, and we couldn't watch TV or play video games. (5) _____ the snow stopped, and the sun came out again. We borrowed some skis and boots from the hotel and went skiing on a summer day!

7A Technology buzzwords

Use four words from the box to correct the underlined mistakes in the sentences.

| apps | the cloud | download | post | spyware | Wi-Fi |

1. My aunt recently started to text her recipes online to share with others. _____
2. Kyle said that a blog was secretly recording my online activity. _____
3. Angela downloaded some podcasts to play games on her smartphone. _____
4. My apartment building has installed a virus, so I can use my laptop anywhere in the building to get on the Internet. _____

7A Expressions for connecting ideas formally

Choose the correct words to complete the text.

Does technology keep you up at night?

Technology has had a positive impact on our lives, for the most part. (1) *Similarly / As a matter of fact / Additionally*, it's hard to imagine how we could live without our computers, smartphones, and apps. These things have made our lives so easy! (2) *Therefore / Nevertheless / As a result*, some technology issues keep me up at night. (3) *Likewise / On the other hand / For example*, what can we do about spyware? As soon as we download software to get rid of it, someone creates a new way to spy on our computers. (4) *For instance / In fact / Furthermore*, there's spyware's nasty cousin, the virus, which can ruin anyone's day. It's a constant battle to overcome these issues, but we can take some common sense steps. Always remember to back up your documents. (5) *In fact / Additionally / As a result*, update your software whenever you get alerts from the manufacturers. Doing these things can help keep technology a positive part of daily life.

7B Words for forms of communication

Cross out the words that do not fit the meaning of the sentences.

A: We're planning an ad campaign to launch a new athletic shoe. In addition to some television ads that look like cool music videos, we'll use (1) *billboards / voice mail / bumper stickers*.

B: Are you also considering (2) *banner ads / pop-up ads / spam* to reach wider audiences?

A: Yes, they're on our list of possibilities. We're also wondering if we should hire a professional basketball player to appear on (3) *a crawl / a bus wrap / an infomercial*.

B: That's a great idea. Now, you may want to know that our research showed that younger audiences think print ads are old-fashioned. They want everything to be digital, so don't use (4) *fliers / billboards / pop-up ads* anymore.

8A Qualities of creative people

Match the correct words to complete the sentences.

1. Nora has the ____f____ to practice daily to achieve her dream of becoming an opera singer.
2. The director was _____ when he chose the actors for the cast. He chose quickly, and didn't ask anyone back for a second audition.
3. Ellie has been on several archeological digs in Asia and is _____ about ancient Chinese and Korean cultures.
4. Pablo is _____ to complete five paintings to enter in the art competition this spring.
5. Gino is _____ in his business; for example, he uses recycled materials to build homes.
6. Chad's science fiction stories are set 500 years in the future and show great _____.

a. decisive
b. resourceful
c. determined
d. knowledgeable
e. originality
f. discipline

8B Collocations for problem solving

Choose the correct words to complete the text.

Groupware

If you ever worked for a multinational company in the past, you know that sometimes it could take hours just to set up a meeting with your colleagues. To help improve productivity, technology companies explored various ways to (1) *find a mistake / (find a solution)* to the problem. They studied the way people worked and (2) *made a mistake / analyzed this information* to figure out how companies might work together more effectively and efficiently. Technological innovators (3) *explored the possibilities of / found problems for* using networked computers and digital office tools. Eventually, they were able to (4) *solve this problem / analyze the problem* by designing groupware, which is software that helps groups of people work together and share information on the Internet. With groupware, colleagues can set up a meeting quickly and have meetings via video, across several continents. And electronic file-sharing systems allow workers to (5) *find alternatives / organize information* and share documents instantly. Problem solved!

9A Expressions related to accepting or changing things

Choose the correct words to complete the conversation.

Amber: I just met your sister. She's so passionate about changing society! She really wants to (1) *follow the crowd* / (*make waves*) / *fit in*.

Becca: Oh yes, Olivia and I are pretty different. I tend to follow the rules and am much more (2) *conventional* / *rebellious* / *unconventional* than she is.

Amber: What was it like growing up in your family? Did your parents teach you to behave yourself and (3) *accept* / *stand up to* / *confront* society's rules?

Becca: Actually, our parents were pretty (4) *unconventional* / *amenable* / *conservative* in their attitudes. At a time when most of their friends were becoming bankers and lawyers, my parents helped set up food pantries to feed poor people in our town.

Amber: Well, that helps explain why Olivia is so active in organizing that free tutoring program at the community center. But why do you think you're so different from her?

Becca: I guess it's just my personality. I want to help people, but I'm kind of shy and don't like to (5) *fit in* / *follow the crowd* / *confront* people.

Amber: I think that's good! You're (6) *being your own person* / *being rebellious* / *making waves* after all.

9B Expressions with *keep* and *stay*

Replace the underlined words in each sentence with an expression from the box above that means the same thing.

| keep in touch | keep out of trouble | keep things in perspective | stay awake |

1. Sofia is moving to a new neighborhood, but her friends hope she will <u>stay connected</u>.

   Sofia is moving to a new neighborhood, but her friends hope she will ___*keep in touch*___.

2. When Pedro gets stressed out about his challenging new job, he tries to <u>remember what's truly important in life</u>.

   When Pedro gets stressed out about his challenging new job, he tries to _____.

| keep connected | keep up with | stay awake | stay out of trouble |

3. Our economics class is difficult, and the professor assigns so many reports and research projects. How do you <u>get it all done</u>?

   How do you _____ it all?

4. Ever since Jack changed schools, he's been hanging out with the wrong crowd. I hope he can <u>avoid getting into a bad situation</u>.

   I hope he can _____.

10A Expressions with *drive*, *get*, and *make*

Cross out the words that do not fit the meaning of the sentences.

Hey, friends, I just returned from a wonderful trip to Bangkok! What amazing street life there! And the food was so spicy and delicious. But traveling there drove (1) *me crazy / me down / me mad*. My flight from Los Angeles was cancelled because of some bad storms. There were long lines to rebook flights, but what made (2) *my blood boil / me mad / on my nerves* was the airline's terrible customer service. It took an hour to get my ticket for a new flight, and then I had to wait two more hours to get through security. Standing in line always gets (3) *me sick / on my nerves / under my skin*. I got stuck behind a family with six noisy, spoiled kids. I was thinking to myself, "Excuse me, but I just used all of my savings for this ticket, and I have to board my flight in 10 minutes!" Talk about driving (4) *someone upset / someone up a wall / someone mad!*

When I finally got on the plane, I ended up sitting next to a guy who kept talking about his big, important job. He bragged so much that it made (5) *my blood boil / me down / me mad*. To get him to stop talking, I pretended to fall asleep. I was so happy when our flight landed!

10B -ed words that describe feelings

Use words from each box to correct the underlined mistakes in the sentences.

baffled   infuriated   insulted

1. Max read over the instructions in his new computer manual several times, but he was still <u>stunned</u>. The instructions were not written very clearly. _____**baffled**_____

2. My boss is impatient and gets angry when she has to wait for things. She was <u>saddened</u> that she had to wait for six months to get a refund for a defective cell phone. _____

3. In some cultures, people feel <u>enraged</u> if new acquaintances refuse to shake hands. _____

frustrated   mystified   stunned

4. Julia was <u>confused</u> because her rent was due on the first of the month, but she wouldn't get her paycheck until the following week. _____

5. After the doctor disappeared, the detective conducted a thorough investigation. Even after analyzing all the evidence, he was still <u>demoralized</u> about what had actually happened. _____

6. Vicky didn't think her violin audition went very well, so she was <u>humiliated</u> to learn that the conductor had selected her for first chair in the orchestra. _____

11A Forming antonyms with prefixes

Choose the true statement for each sentence.

1. Nick thinks it's unethical to tell a white lie, even if it's to protect someone's feelings.
   - ☑ a. Nick thinks it's dishonest to tell a white lie.
   - ☐ b. Nick thinks it's irresponsible to tell a white lie.

2. Mai believes that making wishes is irrational, and that it gives people false hopes.
   - ☐ a. Mai thinks that making wishes is disagreeable.
   - ☐ b. Mai thinks that making wishes is illogical.

3. The accountant is scrupulous about tracking all of the company's profits.
   - ☐ a. The accountant is agreeable.
   - ☐ b. The accountant is responsible.

4. Most lawyers think the judge has a solid reputation for being trustworthy.
   - ☐ a. The judge's behavior is ethical.
   - ☐ b. The judge's behavior is unacceptable.

5. The investigator reported that the bank's lending practices may be unscrupulous.
   - ☐ a. The bank's lending practices may be illegal.
   - ☐ b. The bank's lending practices may be irrational.

6. It's unfair to copy test answers from another student.
   - ☐ a. It's illogical to copy test answers from another student.
   - ☐ b. It's unethical to copy test answers from another student.

11B Adjectives and nouns referring to personal values

Choose the correct words to complete the conversation.

Yoko: One quality I value in my friends is (1) *indifference / selfishness /* (compassion).

Omar: I agree! I also think it's important for friends to be (2) *honest / tender / generous* if they think I'm doing something wrong.

Yoko: It's helpful when my friends are truthful, but I also want them to be (3) *selfish / sensitive / resilient.* I don't want them to hurt my feelings.

Omar: Yeah, I guess that's important. You know, I wish some of my friends were better at keeping secrets! They need to show a little (4) *discretion / kindness / tolerance* when I share something personal.

Yoko: That's true! I expect my friends to have (5) *generosity / resilience / respect* for my privacy. I'm pretty open, but it's annoying when people ask too many questions.

Omar: Yeah, some people are too curious. But, I think overall, my friends are (6) *kind and generous / sensitive and selfish / resilient and indifferent*, and they make me happy!

12A Expressions ending with prepositions

Choose the correct words to complete the email.

Hi Jill,

I heard that you're moving to Tokyo soon to teach English. That's something to (1) *be scared of /* (*be excited about*)!

I remember that when I moved to Buenos Aires last year, it took a while to (2) *get accustomed to / look forward to* a new culture. I had to learn about the way people do business, make friends, and have fun. Luckily, I can speak Spanish, so I was able to (3) *be familiar with / participate in* meetings and conversations. I wanted to (4) *take advantage of / become aware of* cultural events, so I attended concerts, saw plays, and even learned to play guitar from an Argentinean musician!

My advice is to keep an open mind and give yourself time to (5) *adjust to / take advantage of* your new home. And don't (6) *be scared of / become aware of* trying new things.

I (7) *am familiar with / look forward to* hearing about your adventures in Japan!

Henry

12B Compound adjectives

Combine words from the boxes to make compound adjectives to complete the travel tips. Some words will be used more than once. Sometimes more than one answer is possible.

| culturally | non | open | self |

| assured | aware | judgmental | minded | reliant | sensitive |

Travel Tips

1. Be ___*open-minded*___ about trying new kinds of food. You may be captivated by a new cuisine!

2. Be _____ when it comes to exploring places on your own. You want people to think you're a confident, experienced traveler.

3. Be _____ when you experience new cultures. Consider all sides of an issue before forming an opinion.

4. People tolerate different levels of risk. Be _____ and assess your own tolerance for adventure, uncertainty, and possible danger when you plan your trips.

5. If you're traveling on business, learn about local customs and manners and try to be _____ when you meet with clients.

6. If you're going to hike in the mountains, prepare to be _____. Pack essentials such as water, food, rope, maps, a flashlight, and a first-aid kit.

Credits

Illustration credits

Charlene Chua: 8
Jo Goodberry: 20, 40, 60, 86
Brad Hamann: 72
Paul Hostetler: 5, 32, 33, 49, 51, 61, 78
Kim Johnson: 17, 43, 70, 80, 81

Larry Jost: 48
Dan McGeehan: 12, 55, 76, 93
Rob Schuster: 27, 28, 57
Koren Shadmi: 36, 88, 97, 133
James Yamasaki: 42, 82, 90, 104

Photography credits

Back cover: (*clockwise from top center*) ©Leszek Bogdewicz/Shutterstock, ©Wavebreak Media/Thinkstock, ©Blend Images/Alamy, ©limpido/Shutterstock; **2** ©iStock Collection/Thinkstock; **3** (*left to right*) ©iStock Collection/Thinkstock, ©Blend Images/Thinkstock, ©Stockbyte/Thinkstock, ©Digital Vision/Thinkstock; **4** (*top to bottom*) ©Purestock/SuperStock, ©iStock Collection/Thinkstock; **6** (*left to right*) ©Exactostock/SuperStock, ©yu liang wong/Alamy, ©Inmagine/Alamy; **7** ©Monkey Business/Thinkstock; **9** ©Stockbyte/Thinkstock; **10** (*left to right*) ©iStock Collection/Thinkstock, ©iStock Collection/Thinkstock, ©PhotoObjects/Thinkstock; **11** ©I love images/men's lifestyle/Alamy; **13** ©iStock Collection/Thinkstock; **14** (*top to bottom*) ©Gary Lee/Photoshot/Newscom, ©Courtesy of Banksy, ©Lia/Listal, ©Kathy deWitt/Alamy; **15** (*clockwise from top left*) ©Jupiterimages/Thinkstock, ©iStock Collection/Thinkstock, ©PHOTOPQR/L"ALSACE/Newscom; **16** ©NHPA/SuperStock; **18** (*clockwise from top left*) ©eye35.pix/Alamy, ©MIVA Stock/SuperStock, ©JTB PHOTO COMMUNICATI/JTB Photo/SuperStock, ©imagebroker.net/SuperStock; **19** ©Medioimages/Photodisc/Thinkstock; **21** (*top to bottom*) ©Neale Cousland/Shutterstock, ©iStock Collection/Thinkstock; **22** (*left to right*) ©John Foxx/Thinkstock, ©Brian Jannsen/Alamy; **24** (*clockwise from top left*) ©iStock Collection/Thinkstock, ©Jupiterimages/Thinkstock, ©Robert_s/Shutterstock; **25** (*top to bottom*) ©iStock Collection/Thinkstock, ©Hemis.fr/SuperStock; **26** ©Jupiterimages/Thinkstock; **27** (*top to bottom*) ©Blend Images/SuperStock, ©Prisma/SuperStock; **28** (*left to right*) ©Wavebreak Media/Thinkstock, ©iStock Collection/Thinkstock, ©iStock Collection/Thinkstock, ©Comstock/Thinkstock; **29** ©iStock Collection/Thinkstock; **30** ©Wavebreak Media/Thinkstock; **31** ©iStock Collection/Thinkstock; **35** ©iStock Collection/Thinkstock; **37** ©PhotoAlto/SuperStock; **38** (*left to right*) ©Tetra Images/SuperStock, ©Fancy Collection/SuperStock; **39** ©Ryouchin/Getty Images; **40** (*left to right*) ©Comstock/Thinkstock, ©Andrea Morini/Thinkstock, ©iStock Collection/Thinkstock; **44** ©Alain SHRODER/Getty Images; **45** ©iStock Collection/Thinkstock; **46** ©Ammit/Thinkstock; **47** ©Greg Wahl-Stephens/Associated Press; **50** ©Purestock/Thinkstock; **52** ©iStock Collection/Thinkstock; **53** ©Jupiterimages/Thinkstock; **54** ©iStock Collection/Thinkstock; **56** ©iStock Collection/Thinkstock; **58** (*clockwise from top left*) ©Jupiterimages/Thinkstock, ©Creates Images/Thinkstock, ©iStock Collection/Thinkstock, ©Blend Images/SuperStock; **62** (*left to right*) ©iStock Collection/Thinkstock, ©Karen Moskowitz/Getty Images, ©Mircea Bezergheanu/Shutterstock, ©Comstock/Thinkstock; **63** ©Zuma Press, Inc/Alamy; **65** ©iStock Collection/Thinkstock; **66** (*left to right*) ©Ablestock Collection/Thinkstock, ©iStock Collection/Thinkstock, ©You Touch Pix of EuToch/Shutterstock; **67** (*left to right*) ©iStock Collection/Thinkstock, ©Fuse Collection/Thinkstock, ©iStock Collection/Thinkstock; **68** (*left to right*) ©Bloomberg/Getty Images, ©Denise Kappa/Shutterstock; **69** ©Yoshikazu Tsuno/AFP/Getty Images/Newscom; **73** ©meshaphoto/Getty Images; **74** ©Kinga/Shutterstock; **75** (*left to right*) ©Glow Images/Getty Images, ©iStock Collection/Thinkstock, ©Image Source/Thinkstock; **77** (*left to right*) ©prudkov/Shutterstock, ©prudkov/Shutterstock; **79** ©Wavebreak Media/Thinkstock; **84** (*clockwise from top left*) ©Allison Joyce/Stringer/Getty Images, ©iStock Collection/Thinkstock, ©iStock Collection/Thinkstock, ©Stockbyte/Thinkstock, ©GoGo Images Corporations/Alamy, ©mikute/Shutterstock; **87** ©Andrew Vaughan/Associated Press; **91** ©Wavebreak Media/Thinkstock; **92** (*top to bottom*) ©iStock Collection/Thinkstock, ©Jupiterimages/Thinkstock, ©Hemera Collection/Thinkstock, ©Digital Vision/Thinkstock, ©Exactostock/SuperStock, ©iStock Collection/Thinkstock; **94** ©RubberBall/Alamy; **95** ©NY Daily News/Getty Images; **98** (*top to bottom*) ©Harry How/Staff/Getty Images, ©Robin Smith/Getty Images; **100** ©Design Pics/SuperStock; **101** (*left to right*) ©Belinda Images/SuperStock, ©frans lemmens/Alamy, ©I love images/city break/Alamy; **102** (*left to right*) ©iStock Collection/Thinkstock, ©Top Photo Group/Thinkstock, ©iStock Collection/Thinkstock; **103** ©Morgan David de Lossy/Corbis; **130** ©AFP/Getty Images; **135** ©Aurora Photos/Alamy; **137** ©Cultura Creative/Alamy; **141** ©Michael Coyne/Getty Images

Text credits

The authors and publishers acknowledge the following sources of copyright material and are grateful for the permissions granted. While every effort has been made, it has not always been possible to identify the sources of all the material used, or to trace all copyright holders. If any omissions are brought to our notice, we will be happy to include the appropriate acknowledgments on reprinting.

9 Adapted from "My Tribe," by Erin Peterson, *Experience Life*, September 2005. Reproduced with permission of Erin Peterson; **17** Adapted from "Amnesia Spoils Newlyweds' Bliss," *ABC News*, June 30, 2005. Reproduced with permission of ABC News; **43** Adapted from "What Type of Cell Phone User Are You?" by Nancy Friedman. Reprinted with permission of Telephone Doctor Customer Service Training in St. Louis, MO. Nancy Friedman, President, is a keynote speaker at association meetings and Chamber of Commerce events as well as corporate gatherings. Call 314.291.1012 for more information or visit the website at www.telephonedoctor.com; **61** Adapted from "Brother, can you spare a dime for my Gucci bills?" by Janelle Brown, *Salon*, October 2, 2002. This article first appeared in Salon.com, at www.salon.com. An online version remains in the Salon archives. Reprinted with permission; **69** Adapted from "Mr. Song and Dance Man," by Dr. David McNeill, *Japan Focus*. Reproduced with permission of Dr. David McNeill, Sophia University, Tokyo; **77** Adapted from "4 Ways to Brush Up Your Problem-Solving Skills," by Barbara T. Armstrong, October 24, 2012. Reproduced with permission of Barbara T. Armstrong, Kahler Slater, Inc.; **87** Adapted from "Dave Carroll is still having problems with airlines," by Ellen Roseman, *The Toronto Star*, May 18, 2012. Reprinted with permission of Torstar Syndication Services; **103** Adapted from "Get Yourself Lost," by Arthur Frommer, *Travel Holiday*, September 1994.

Answers

Page 44, Exercise 1B: Story 3 is false.